This book is dedicated to the firefighters we've lost within our fire family.

We carry you with us in our hearts and our stories.

For firefighters, by firefighters,
in support of firefighters:

The fire family is just that, *family.* It's part of our ethos
to take care of our own. With that in mind, a portion
of this book's proceeds will go to organizations that
assist wildland firefighters and their families when
they need it most.

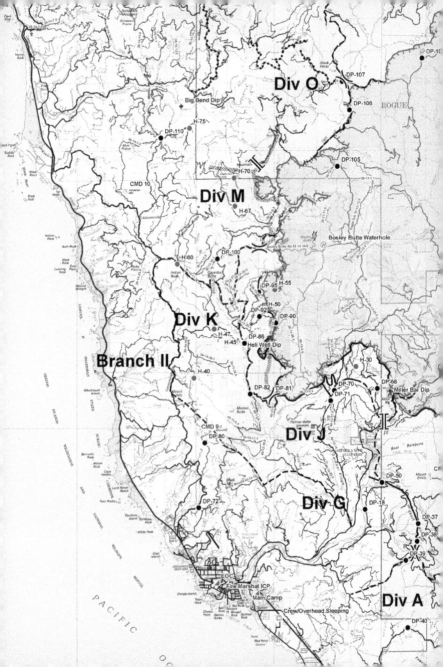

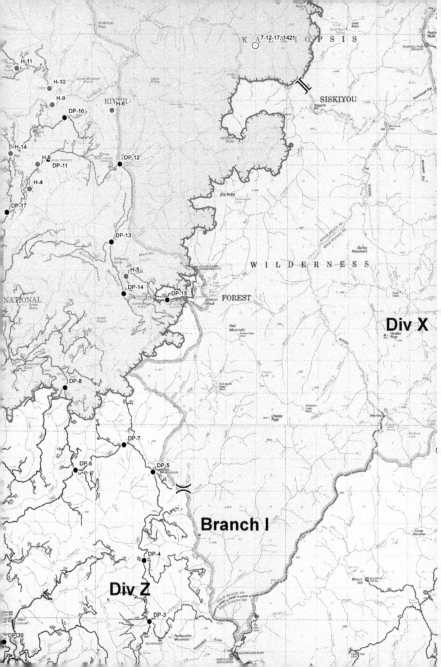

HOLD AND IMPROVE

A collection of awesomeness
from the edge of the fireline

CONTENTS

Chapter 4: Ponderings   96

INTRODUCTION

Once I got into wildland firefighting it didn't take me very long to realize that this work isn't for everyone, in fact, *it's hardly for anyone.* However, for the select few who truly get this job and find it second nature to endure the harsh environment, the relentless physicality, and the relatively consistent discomfort associated, well, the rewards are intangible at best. But the repayment shows up in ways difficult to imagine.

This line of work fills people with a sense of purpose and pride. It folds them into the unshakeable camaraderie of the fire family and drops them into places so secluded they'd swear they were the only people to have ever touched that piece of earth. The job will push someone to the furthest ends of their physical and mental capacity, as they simultaneously witness beauty so profound it's simply unspeakable. And perhaps above all else, this profession offers the exceedingly rare and distinct honor of living among the elements.

Wildland firefighters are connected to, and acutely aware of our natural surroundings in a way that few in this modern-day era ever will be. We take quick notice of shifts in wind direction, cloud types, rises in humidity, and inversion layers. We squeeze pinecones and crunch leaves in our hands to feel their moisture content or lack thereof. We make beds in the dirt and arise to ridgetop views. When all aspects of the job converge, it begins to make sense why time spent on the fireline results in some of the fondest experiences of a lifetime.

One major component of the wildfire culture is, and always has been, storytelling. While some of the best storytelling is done around a warming fire or during mop-up, the community has other outlets. There are places for wildland firefighters to share perspectives about teamwork or leadership and spaces to offer lessons learned or share personal accounts of traumatic situations; there are even platforms to advocate for reform. However, what's been missing is a home to celebrate the seemingly intangible aspects of why we do this job in the first place. And so, that's what this is.

Hold and Improve is a tribute to the fire family and the storytelling culture within it. Between the covers of this book you'll find a collection of short stories, artwork, poetry, and more. All of which, were born from the hearts, minds, and experiences of wildland firefighters. The true stories shared here are relatable to a degree that it captures the essence of camaraderie on paper, while the poetry and artwork highlight the multi-faceted talents of the fire family.

The title of this book -*Hold and Improve*- is derived from the fireline. "Hold and Improve" is a familiar message passed down the line from one firefighter to the next, signifying the need to stop forward movement and improve the piece of fireline where you are. Over time the command has also turned into a catchphrase for moments when firefighters are asked to sit idle just waiting to engage. It's moments like these when you might see a firefighter pull out a badly misshapen book from the depths of their fire pack to help them pass the time. It could be mere minutes or several hours before being called to leap back into action. *Hold and Improve* is comprised of short stories so that at the very least, it will give firefighters a fighting chance to finish reading a story before being summonsed into line order once again.

I realize you may be thinking, "If this book is meant to be on the fireline, why does it have a white cover?"

The white cover provides a blank canvas for you to leave your mark on this book. The addition of your ash-stained fingerprints on the cover is welcome and encouraged. *Hold and Improve* will not be offered in digital form because the physical experience of holding a book in your hands cannot be supplemented with a virtual substitute. And just as we share stories around the warming fire, this book can be shared too. Why not inscribe your name and the year you read it on the inside cover, then pass it off and see how far the fire world takes it? While you're at it, feel free to use the blank pages and wide margins to scribble out whatever inspires you.

When the idea for this book first came to me, I envisioned a new volume of *Hold and Improve* being released annually. The fire community is chock-full of intriguing stories and incredible talent, far exceeding the capacity of just one volume. So, if you're a wildland firefighter (past or present) and have something you'd like to share, keep an eye out for the next submission period, which is set to take place each fall.

And now I'd like to extend kind greetings to all of you readers who aren't firefighters but have an interest in what the fire world is like. Thank you for deciding to pick up this book.

Before diving in, it's important to note that the fire community essentially has its own language. The stories within *Hold and Improve -Volume Alpha-* are written in much the same manner that they'd be told out in the field around a warming fire. Because of this, I have provided a glossary of terms at the back of the book. The glossary is there to help ensure that even if you've never fought fire, you'll still be able to easily follow along. Surely rookie firefighters will get good use out of the glossary of terms as well.

I reckon it's about time for me to bring this introduction to a close. But first, I'd like to offer my wholehearted appreciation to the fire community for helping spread the word about this project while offering me words of encouragement, and most importantly, for sending submissions to include in the book. *Hold and Improve* would never have come to fruition without you.

Cheers-
Bre Orcasitas

CHAPTER 1
BACK IN THE DAY

"Crown Fire Smoke" Charcoal from an Arizona Wildfire
Size: 16 x 12" By Stephanie Peters

The Legend of Ed Pulaski

Story by: Bre Orcasitas

There are countless variations to the story about to be told, but that's how legends are born, through first-hand accounts being told and re-told by others until the story is larger than life.

In the early 1900s, Ed Pulaski found himself working as a U.S. Forest Service Ranger in Wallace, Idaho. Those who lived in his era witnessed the Great Fire of 1910 with their own eyes, and if they were lucky, they lived to tell about it. The "Big Burn" as it would later be called, consumed a large portion of forests across the West and beyond, simultaneously reducing entire towns to ash.

On August 20th, while Ed Pulaski and nearly 150 others were staffing multiple fires in the forest near Wallace, the weather took a turn. The winds were so strong that Ed Pulaski would later say they were like, "a terrific hurricane so strong it almost lifted men out of their saddles." The winds had significantly intensified the fire activity and so, Pulaski gathered up the men he was working with, about 45 or so, and began to lead them through the forest back to Wallace.

However, Ed Pulaski and his men became trapped between a backburn lit by the residents of Wallace, and the fire they had just abandoned. With no-way-out, Ed Pulaski would have to think fast.

Having been a prospector prior to working as a ranger, Pulaski had intricate knowledge of all the nearby prospector tunnels in the immediate area. He managed to convince his men to join him in the Nicholson tunnel just before the fire front reached their location. As the fire roared just outside, the tunnel quickly filled with smoke and intense heat. Ed Pulaski urged his men to lie face down in a little stream to protect themselves from gas and smoke but some panicked and tried to run out into the flames. That's when Pulaski stopped them in their tracks by holding them at gunpoint. He said that being shot by him would be a much kinder death than the one waiting for them outside the tunnel.

Eventually, the conditions inside the tunnel became so intense that every person lost consciousness. One firefighter awoke several hours later and managed to make his way to Wallace for help. A crew was quickly assembled for a rescue mission and when they returned to find Ed Pulaski lying face down and unconscious someone uttered, "Boys, the boss is dead." To which they heard Pulaski reply, "Like hell he is."

All but a few of the men managed to survive, and Ed Pulaski would forever carry the weight of those losses with him, even after having saved so many.

Ed Pulaski continued to work for the U.S. Forest Service after the Big Burn. In fact, just a few years later, after endlessly tinkering with prototypes, he created the single most valuable asset any wildland firefighter has in their repertoire… *the pulaski*. The pulaski tool is part axe, part adze hoe, and entirely awesome. The invention of the pulaski tool is akin to the Model-T in the world of automobiles; whatever came before is inconsequential because the invention was so revolutionary. There truly is no equal to the diversity of the pulaski as a firefighting tool. But should that be surprising? Firefighters know what they need, and they are skilled enough to create their own solutions rather than waiting around for someone else to do it.

So, if you ever find yourself in the quaint town of Wallace, Idaho perhaps you might want to pay a visit to the original pulaski tool, complete with Ed Pulaski's initials carved into the handle. I have stood before that original pulaski, studying it intensely, trying to assess what changes have been made over the years from its original design. After looking closely, I've come to the conclusion that those slight alterations away from his design are doing a disservice to firefighters. That guy knew what he was doing.

Now, there are those who make claims that someone else came up with the pulaski design and that Ed Pulaski merely improved on that prototype. *Well, see, that's the thing about legends;* there are always countless variations to be told... and that version of the story gets no play here.

Dead Doug Fir

Story by: Bobbie Scopa

It was 1974, and I was the newest member of a start-up hotshot crew. Back then we were inter-regional hotshot crews. Of course, I had no idea what any of that meant, because this was my first summer on a crew and I was their last hire of the season. Apparently, they lost someone else and as a last resort -and at the urging of a friend of mine already on the crew- they hired me.

I was unprepared for life on a hotshot crew because I didn't even know what it meant to fight a wildland fire. Did we use hoses like a city fire engine? Did we hike a lot? I was in for a hard miserable summer but didn't know it yet. By the time I arrived in the small mountain mining town with a ranger station, the fire training had already been completed. I wouldn't even get a basic explanation of our job and what I should do. On my first day on the job, I was even told they had no line gear for me to use.

"You'll have to go to an Army surplus store and buy some webbing, canteens and a small pack to carry your gear", the crew boss told me. Everyone else had already gotten their gear from the agency. *Ok, no problems.* I was just happy and excited to be a firefighter... whatever that meant. I was already an experienced backpacker so it wouldn't be hard to figure out what I needed.

Very quickly I learned that the crew boss didn't like me. He hated when I asked questions, and I asked *lots and lots* of questions. Of course I had questions! I had no idea what cutting a fireline had to do with putting out a brush fire in chaparral. Without the basic training that all rookie firefighters go through, how was I to know? During training exercises I'd ask,

Uh, why are we cutting this trail? What does this have to do with putting out the fire?

"Shut up, Scopa!"

But I was just wondering.....

"Shut up and DIG!"

And that's how my first summer of fighting fire went. But I loved the physical aspect of the job. I loved being outdoors, sharpening my assigned tools, hiking, and I absolutely loved fighting fire. I already knew my future was not going to be on this crew, so I would pick up what I could by watching, and then move on to another crew next year, but for now I was going to have some fun and learn on my own. There were some good guys on that crew. I felt safe and friendly with some of them, but I was an outsider compared to all the locals. But no worries, I would stick it out because I was more stubborn than they were. But how to survive?

Uh, do the guys on the fire engine cut line too?

"I said shut up, Scopa!"

But I was just curious...

"SHUT UP AND DIG."

Slowly, I learned I could get some satisfaction from asking dumb questions of the crew boss. The more questions I asked, the hotter the crew boss got. Most of my questions were legit but some were asked just to get a reaction. I'd act all innocent when I was asking the questions, but in reality, I got some enjoyment from pissing him off. I already knew he couldn't stand me, so if I could get a giggle from my fellow crew members when they saw him get mad, that was satisfying in an odd sort of way. I was already on his shit list. I might as well enjoy the ride!

One evening, the crew went out for beer and pizza. In a very rough town, you didn't go out to a bar by yourself if you didn't want to get beaten up or worse. Those evenings that the crew went out for a beer together made me feel like I was really out with my brothers. While drinking pitchers of beer one night, we started arm wrestling. No one thought I'd be any good, but I won a few rounds. Then it was my turn to take on the crew boss. We were both already under the influence when he sneered at me and said, "OK, Scopa, your turn."

I didn't say anything. I had no thought that I could beat the almighty crew boss in an arm-wrestling contest. He was a tough guy who'd been a firefighter for a long time and I was the lowest member on the crew. I sat down across from him while the crew all stood around the table, which was covered with pitchers of beer and half-full glasses. He had that same old goofy look on his face that he always had. He hated me and I wasn't too fond of him either, but he had all the power. Well, he did, but not that night. That night I beat him in an arm-wrestling contest.

The crew erupted and the crew boss jumped up completely pissed off.

"I can't believe it... I can't believe it. This is bullshit! How could Scopa beat me!?! Bullshit!"

Heck, I couldn't believe it either. I just stood up with a big smile on my face amazed about what had just happened. I didn't say anything. I just walked around the bar while everyone slapped me on my back. I had gained some status on the crew that night. But by the next day, I'd be lower than whale shit on the bottom of the ocean again.

One of the projects our crew worked on while not assigned to a fire was building a barbed wire fence around a recreation site near town on top of a steep mountain. We worked on that project all summer; cutting juniper for posts and carrying them up and down slopes so steep we were often on our hands and knees. Digging holes for the corner posts and H-braces was like digging through solid rock. You know how that can be. It's hard work.

Now that the entire crew had watched me beat the crew boss at an arm-wrestling contest, the crew boss was being particularly nasty to me. Not too far out of his normal, but I couldn't even get a civil response to any comment or question I might have. Even if those questions were about how a particular H-brace was to be built or how tight the barbed wire was supposed to be. Now, even legitimate questions were scoffed at, the familiar response rang in my ear.

"Shut up, Scopa!"

At this point it became comical. My fellow firefighters began to laugh and roll their eyes when they heard the crew boss yell at me. One day, during lunch while on this project we sat around telling stories and laughing at each other's misfortunes of bruised knuckles and torn jeans from the arduous work. As is often the case, hard work can be a team building experience. This was that opportunity and the crew was enjoying the cool shade and relaxation before we went back to an afternoon's toil.

While we were all relaxing, the crew boss made a comment that my smart-ass self just had to respond to. I just couldn't pass up an opportunity to mess with the boss. He had been ridiculing me all summer and then I had the audacity to beat him in an arm-wrestling contest? How dare I! The crew boss wasn't the smartest fella, so all I had to do was be subtle with my comments. All these years later I don't remember what he said and how I responded, but I made sure it was a delicate attack on his intelligence. I assumed he wouldn't get the joke but if he did get it, I knew I'd be in big trouble.

Luckily, the verbal jab went right over his head, but that wasn't the case for everyone. A few of my friends started laughing and looking at me. That gave it away. He knew something was up and looked from face to face trying to figure out the joke. I assumed my innocent face and looked back at him. All of a sudden his face changed, he got the joke. *Oh no, I'm in trouble now.*

"Scopa, you think you're so smart? I've got a project for you. After lunch you can take down that Doug fir snag."

Next to our lunch spot was a Doug fir snag that had been dead for many years. It was hard as a rock and about 6 feet in diameter.

I get to cut that down? Awesome!

In all my time on the crew, they never once let me touch a chainsaw and for some reason I thought all of a sudden, the crew boss was going to let me drop a huge dangerous snag. Forget all the environmental and safety red flags this would raise, this was a chance to drop a monster tree my first time with a saw! But of course, he had no intention of letting me use a chain saw, there's status in using a chainsaw and he would be conferring no status to me that afternoon.

"No chainsaw. You're going to drop it with your pulaski."

Everyone on the crew started snickering and laughing under their breath. No one wanted to get involved and incur the wrath of the crew boss, but one of my friends was now laughing out loud, and was quickly singled out by the crew boss.

"You, Smith. You're going to help. The two of you drop that snag after lunch... with your pulaskis."

The entire crew was laughing at us. How could we possibly drop a 6' DBH hard-as-a-rock snag with our pulaskis?

The crew stood around and watched as we sized up the tree before hiking off to work on the fence for the afternoon. The tree was so big that one of us could start hacking at the face cut while the other worked on the back cut. The tree was so large we couldn't even see each other while swinging our pulaskis. My face cut had to have been close to two feet tall and my arms felt like they were falling off from the fatigue of wailing away on that old tree. We'd stop to sharpen our tools and rest our arms every so often. We were sweaty and tired but amazed that our old "project" pulaskis had cut as much wood as they had. But after a few hours of this I had to swing from my waist to get the pulaski to move at all. It was as if my arms had turned into wet noodles.

By now, the crew had reassembled at the lunch spot waiting for us to finish the job. We'd been cutting on this behemoth for over three hours and there was still at least three feet of holding wood. My face cut was the ugliest you'd ever seen. Imagine a beaver with dull teeth gnawing at a giant tree; that was my face cut. On top of how ugly it was, my arms wouldn't be usable for days. Now everyone was getting antsy because they wanted to get back down the mountain to refurb before it got too late. But the crew boss wanted to extract his due for a bit longer.

Finally, when he saw our progress had slowed to some miserable little chips coming out of our mining operation he called one of the sawyers over to finish our job. This ancient tree that had been standing for a few centuries, came down after a couple minutes of saw work. I was happy to be done with that one.

I managed to finish the season with that crew, but I think they were just as happy to be rid of me as I was to move on. I went on to have a long career in the fire service, but I still smile and laugh when I remember peppering that crew boss with questions, some innocent, some not. I laugh at the memories of trying to look and act innocent that summer while also trying *unsuccessfully* to fit in.

I learned a lot that summer. I learned what not to do on a crew and with a crew boss that didn't like me. Even though I never received any formal training, I learned a lot about fire tactics and line construction. I even learned about leadership, because you can learn a lot whether the leader is a good one or not. But I learned a lot about me too. One thing I learned that summer is that a good laugh is worth a few days of limp noodle arms.

"Smoke in the Field" Charcoal
Size: 7 x 9" By Stephanie Peters

Bear Bait

Story by: Dee Townsend

Napi Point Fire, St. Maries, MT (1984)

O ur hotshot crew ended up dispatched to a fire at the edge of Glacier National Park in late August of '84. Now, in recent years, some women had been mauled by Grizzly bears in Glacier NP and wildlife biologists had attributed it to the **possibility** that *perhaps* they were menstruating. So, there we were in bear country, and I was one of two women on the 20-person crew.

As we arrived to the fire we were placed on night shift. A few shifts into our fire assignment, somewhere around midnight, my squad boss came to let me know a guy needed to talk with me. *Why?* I asked and he replied, "About your condition... your period." Now, mind you, this was month four of being on the crew and everyone knew everything about what is going on in your life. Not to mention I had been popping pills due to bad cramps while digging line over the past couple of days. *Great.* I said to him.

So, my squaddie and I walked down the fireline to where

some of my crew and a stranger were standing. I waited, but no one said anything for about 5 minutes. I finally asked the stranger if he wanted to talk with me. He fumbled, stuttered, and finally spit out, "uh, yes." *OKAAAAYYYY then?* I decide to make it easy for the dude. I told him the answer to the magic question of this evening was, *yes*. He explained his bear attack concerns and informed me as well as my crew overhead that he needed to escort me back to camp per direction from the fire's incident management team (IMT).

The hike out was about 3 miles. It was night, and the idiot didn't bring any bear spray or a gun, so instead of being around a crew of 20 people running pumps, saws, and tools, this dude and I hiked through a dark forest in silence. Prime bear bait if you ask me, given the specialist's "theory." Fortunately, we arrived safely at his vehicle and then began the drive to fire camp, which was another 20 miles. Along the way, we met other fire-related vehicles some of which, were his buddies or fire teammates, and he proceeded to tell each and every one of them why he was taking me back to camp. I was becoming more humiliated and disgusted with each passing mile; sitting there fuming in silence.

Back at camp, I asked to be given work since I was wide

awake after having been on several nightshifts at this point. The temperatures were in the mid-20s so the last thing I wanted to do was lay wide-awake shivering in my sleeping bag and plastic hooch (no tents were issued in 1984). The guy couldn't find any camp work so he decided that a short-staffed engine crew that was assigned closer to civilization and working off a road might be a safe place for me. He dropped me off with the engine crew (who happened to be from our neighboring forest back home) and I was put to work at the end of a hose lay, mopping up.

A few hours later, sometime near dawn, the engine captain called for a break and a warm-up in the engine. During our break, the captain eventually asked me, "What's wrong with you? Why are you here with us? You don't look hurt, and I know the shot crew would not let you off the crew otherwise. So, what's up?"

I replied with a question myself,

Shall I be polite or blunt with my answer?

He said, "It's 5 am. We've been working all night. Blunt works."

Ok, I paused, *I'm on the rag and the fire team is afraid that*

the bears are going to get me.

He exclaimed, "Well shit! If I had known that I wouldn't have put you at end of the hose lay so far away from the engine!" We carried on, laughing about it over our coffee.

The next night I was back with my hotshot crew. (I don't know why the team's "direction" changed in less than 24 hours? Maybe the bears were given a safety briefing about the consequences of human interactions.) Our foreman asked, "Who will work with Dee?" After a few minutes of hesitation, the "old man" of the crew (by shot crew standards anyhow) grabbed a chainsaw, fired it up, and said, "I will, no problem." Baited for bear indeed!

There were other crews on that fire with women who had to deal with the same situation as me. As a matter of fact, almost an entire squad on another shot crew were "rescued" by the incident management team. All of us were eventually given the nickname "Bear Bait." And while bears *did* move back into the fire area when things cooled off, my crew never saw any; even with all the "bait."

Karma in an Oyster Tin

Story by: Riva Duncan

When I was on a hotshot crew I was in complete awe of the foreman (today's equivalent of a squad leader). He was larger than life in my eyes; a wiry guy who could crank out pull-ups and push-ups like no one else, and he ran like a jack rabbit. He was a quiet leader and had been on engines, crews, and had also been a helicopter rappeller. He was a great teacher, a natural. I never once heard him raise his voice, yet he could silence someone with just a look. A look that I never wanted to be the un-lucky recipient of. (But of course, I was... several times.) He seemed to be always watching, thinking, anticipating, and planning. I really wanted his approval; I wanted him to think me worthy of not just being a wildland firefighter, but a hotshot as well.

It was still early in the season and we'd been out on several prescribed burns in a couple different states before being assigned to some fires in Texas. Conditions had moderated in Texas, and so when our home unit busted a big fire, we got reassigned and hit the road, driving all day. Our assign-ment was two-fold; to pull-off a large burn-out operation on a section of the fire while the burning conditions were favorable, and then tie into the dozer line with handline while also prepping roads for a later burn-out.

I hadn't been feeling well on the long drive and was fighting nausea but I didn't tell anyone. As a wildland firefighter it's pretty normal not to speak up about illness or injuries and to power through instead. I didn't want to just sit in the truck while everyone got to fight fire, especially on what looked to be a pretty sweet assignment. And of course, no one wants to miss out on overtime and hazard pay.

We jumped out of the trucks, grabbed tools, got our briefing, and started a fast hike up a very steep-ass mountain to the ridge top. We could see the glow of the fire waiting for us in the distance. We powered past a job corps crew and several other resources and stopped once we crested the ridge. While the supt. and asst. supt. developed a plan, I stood sweating and fighting the urge to vomit. Steve walked back from the front of the line, stopped in front of me and asked,

"What's wrong with you?"

I feel sick. I think I'm going to puke.

To which he replied, "Get the hell out of the line and go over there in the brush if you're going to puke," pointing off to the left. I scrambled into the bushes, threw down my tool, and dropped to my knees, my arms wrapped around my middle. I didn't even bother taking off my line pack, I only unbuckled the waist strap. Suddenly, Steve was on his knees next to me. He leaned forward and got into my face, looking me in the eyes before he said, "I thought you had to puke. C'mon, puke. I want to see chunks come out of your mouth. What are you waiting for?"

I've never wanted to vomit so badly in my life, and right in his face would have been amazing, but all I could do was dry-heave. He stood up and said with disgust, "Get your ass back in line."

So, I stumbled back into line and carried on.

We worked hard all night, successfully pulling off the big burn-out with only a few small spot fires. At about 0300 the supt. told us to take a break, and grab some food. We built a big warming fire and sprawled out around it as people dug into their packs for food. The supt. presented a can of smoked oysters asking, "Anyone want these? Riv?"

Now, I love smoked oysters. Like Bubba loves shrimp, I love

all oysters and normally I would've snatched that tin up, but I still felt like shit. The thought of eating them made my stomach flip-flop. *I'll pass, my stomach is still jacked up,* I said.

"I'll take them," said Steve. Some folks ate, some hunkered down close to the fire and dozed, some did both. After way too short of a break we got back to work. Narwhal took my squad to construct that last piece of fireline, while Steve took the other squad to patrol and mop up the area we had burned out.

A few hours later, after daybreak, we had a good fireline completed. As I was hiking down the line, one of the guys from the other squad called me over. "Hey, Riva, come over here! You gotta see this."

I walked over to where he stood, on a vantage point above a forest road. Once I got close, he pointed down below toward the road and there was Steve. He was lying in the brush on a switch-back, curled up in the fetal position. His yellow shirt was hiked up around his waist, and his Nomex pants and boxers were pushed down around his ankles. His skinny bare ass shone as white as a beacon. *What the hell?* I asked.

"You know those oysters that the supt. gave him? Well, they must've been bad because he's been puking and shitting himself for about an hour."

Holy fuck. I said, trying really hard not to laugh. Trucks drove right past Steve and he didn't even care. My buddy and I high-fived.

Steve and I actually became really close friends after my time on the crew and always stayed in touch. After a few different gigs, a different hotshot crew, more rappelling, and a district AFMO job, Steve went back to that crew as the assistant supt. and then moved up to superintendent. Nearly twenty years later, when I ended up being hired as a Forest FMO, I hired Steve off the crew as my assistant FFMO. We had a blast working together and made a good team. I loved to tell that story, and he loved it too. We'd laugh, people would shake their heads, and Steve would say, with a grin on his face, "Man, I was such an asshole then."

And I'd say, with a grin on my face, *Karma, baby. Karma.*

"She'll Survive" Watercolor
by Tonja Opperman

Binkies, Blankies, and Binoculars

Story by: Bequi Livingston

It was 0230 hours on June 13, 1998 and my work cell phone was ringing. All I could think was, *Shit! Another fire in the Sandia Mountains while my husband is out of town for work and I'm here alone with the kids.* I answered the phone to hear dispatch on the other end telling me that the citywide 911 system had been inundated with phone calls regarding a fire on the west slopes of the Sandias, which are located in Albuquerque's backyard, visible to the entire metropolitan area. As the district's assistant fire management officer (AFMO), this was on my watch tonight. Begrudgingly, I got up, got dressed, and woke my two kids (ages 4 and 8), telling them that we were going out to find a fire. By now, they knew this drill by heart. My daughter with her blankie, my son with his binkie, and me with my binoculars, all loaded into the minivan and headed for the foothills to find a good vantage point to try and confirm the smoke report.

We parked at the Elena Gallegos Open Space, which gave us a great view of the fire -a single tree- burning in steep terrain about halfway up the mountain; which looked enormous to the residents of Albuquerque. We sat in the van for about an hour, each of us with our own pair of binoculars, watching the fire as it slowly subsided into nothingness. *Whew!* I thought. Another lucky strike, because the west side of the Sandia Mountains had been primed to burn for decades – but thankfully, not tonight. By now, both kids were sound asleep in their car seats, as we started our drive back home. This sort of seemingly rare experience (dragging your kids out of bed in search of a new fire start) had become "ops normal" for me as a fire mom, and life would continue on that way for 20+ years, but looking back now I have to say, I wouldn't have had it any other way.

I knew the day my daughter was born that my first priority and my strongest passion was being a mother, priority number two being wildfire. Of course, I was lucky that my dual career husband (a helicopter pilot whom I'd met on a fire in Colorado) equally valued and prioritized spending quality time with our children. We had made a pact early in our marriage, that no matter what the demands of our jobs were, one of us would always be at home with the kids. That meant that sometimes I'd literally have to leave an initial attack fire (IA) in order to pick the kids up from daycare before it closed, and that was okay because, well, it had to be.

As the kids got older our daughter began year-round

softball and would spend her summers playing on travel teams, which meant that instead of my summers being spent on various fire assignments or supporting local wildfires, I'd use annual leave to travel with my daughter for softball. Luckily, through the years, no matter my position in fire, management always supported my family's needs, mostly because they themselves were parents or grandparents, and they understood the challenges. Those of us who are fire parents know all the other facets that accompany this wonderful journey; including times when our children get sick and we need to stay home with them, or when their afterschool care is randomly cancelled and we need to drop everything to go and pick them up. Along with being a firefighter 24/7/365, we are parents 24/7/365, and that will always take precedence.

During stretches of the fire season when I'd have to work weekends my kids would come along if my husband was out of town. That happened many, many times. My co-workers were always supportive and would help to 'entertain' my children while I worked; pushing them down the slick halls in chairs on wheels, even allowing them to color on the walls of the building (with a full remodel right around the corner, why not?) to pass some time. And if any kids ever felt like they were close personal friends with

Smokey Bear, it was certainly ours; having happily joined the Smokey Bear Club and getting unique opportunities to accompany Smokey on school visits.

For several years we took our annual family photo that we used for our Christmas cards in the helicopter that my husband piloted. Whenever I look back at those pictures I'm always reminded of the special moments we all shared along the way, and it leaves me filled with gratitude that my children were able to be part of my fire career. Which brings me back to that summer evening in 1998; my kids in the van with me, scouting for fires in the Sandia Mountains, and I think, *how lucky can one get?* Going to scout fires with binkies, blankies and binoculars! It doesn't get much better than that, now does it?

2015

POLLOCK Mountain
Lookout

.... the humble majesty of mountains,
their secrets reveal themselves slowly as the
light shifts. Raspberries ripen as i sit, still as
lichen on a rock, letting the sun scan my whole being
inside out, as it sets behind my back. the full face
of the blue moon grinning back at me eye level
elevation. how dark was the night? very. except for
the blinding brilliance of countless stars. busy
pikas barking on the basalt. they hope for the future.
stashing hay in leiu of hibernation. bouquets of
sulphur flowers in their mouths, the farmers of the
high country. "the essential sometimes hangs by a thread."
dont cut your eyes on craggy peaks. a storm approaches.
giant jellyfish virga clouds, dragging themselves slowly,
rumbling, rumbling across canyons echos. thunder, feels
like a magnent as it passes over. electricity streaks
cloud to cloud, crooked arrows meet their mark, smell
of wet sage, soak into your pores, rainbows that can
only be seen by you. lightning strikes like intuition.
sometimes, ideas catch on fire immeaditly, others take
awhile wind to flare up. smoldering trees, inscence to the
universe. everything changes. every day is different, a
constant suprise with sun rise. time and space, light on
your face, the movements of your soul stirring with
the seasons. Reality Real estate. the heart is a
drunken compass. happy trails to you, until we meet
again. GRAtitude ~~~> xoxo
                          Laura grace

Prose of a Lookout by: Lookout Laura

CHAPTER 2
ENCOUNTERS WITH THE ANIMAL KINGDOM

"Fire Notebook" Pen
by Anonymous

Bullwinkle

Story by: Steve Holdsambeck

It was July 1978, I had just turned 20 and was a co-op
student with the Talladega National Forest majoring in
forestry attending Auburn University. I had been on lots
of (maybe a hundred?) local fires, with almost all of them
referred to as nuisance fires set by trash burners or turkey
and raccoon hunters. I had heard and read about the "campaign fires" of the West and was anxious to one day get on
one of those 'real' fires; an exciting fire. Then finally, my
time had come.

The ranger mustered up a 20-person crew to be led by a
tobacco chewing, fifty-something embodiment of a red
neck (including actually having a perpetually sun-burned
neck). This crewboss -a timber marker in real life- was a
nice guy generally, but in his role as crewboss, he took on
the attitude of a Marine drill sergeant.

Leaving Talladega very early the next morning, in vans and
pickups, we met up with other crews in Montgomery, Alabama. We spent the entire day at the airport having been
told that our plane would arrive shortly, and if we weren't

ready, we'd get left. Just before dark, we packed into a jet that had "TWA" sanded off and painted over on the side of the plane. The pilot advised that we were headed to Boise, Idaho but would need to stop in Kansas along the way to refuel due to weight limits. The crewboss briefed that we were headed to "BIFC," the Boise Interagency Fire Center.

Several of the Alabama firefighters had never been on a plane before, and as it struggled to make lift-off speed, there began a memorable cacophony of hymns, screams, and prayers. I don't think Jesus had any choice but to be in that cockpit after having been summoned so intensely.

Landing in Boise just after sunrise, we hiked across the tarmac to the BIFC mess hall, where we were given sleeves of ham sandwiches and bags full of candy which, evidently fulfilled our breakfast, lunch, and dinner allotment. Nearby, several water buffalos were available to fill canteens. There were probably a thousand other firefighters there in the ever apparent logistical nightmare. I recall that there was no shade available anywhere, and by noon it was brutally hot in the sun. Our crew was confined to a patch of grass and told to wait for further instructions.

The sun, the heat, and the boredom were only made acceptable somehow because a thousand others also had to endure it; like some kind of mass psychological control technique. Everyone was exhausted, but with no shade, it was too hot to sleep. Experienced firefighters were those who had a paperback to read or a deck of cards.

Finally, the shadows began to lengthen and firefighters from other crews started unrolling paper sleeping bags that had somehow appeared. Soon the boss told us to line up to get a sleeping bag, so we trailed over to the giant BIFC cache warehouse. A steady stream of firefighters came out of the warehouse with sleeping bags under their arms but still hundreds more firefighters waited in line. After an hour or so, the boss advised they had run out of sleeping bags and reminded us that, "complainers can go home." So, we tramped back over to our grass patch and tried to make a bed out of our clothes. As it got dark, the noise of generators began to dominate all other sounds and massive stadium lights were turned on, which brought perfect daytime visibility to a thousand firefighters trying desperately to get some sleep.

Eventually, I dozed off only to be startled awake by scores of firefighters cussing and screaming, then almost simultaneously, I felt the cold spray of automatic sprinklers. The crewboss barked orders for us to gather at an adjacent parking lot and later barked that he would not tolerate complainers. He also said that experienced firefighters know to eat, sleep and shit every chance they get, "so get to sleep!" That little nugget of wisdom stuck with me my whole career.

Just before sunrise, the execrable stadium lights and generators started turning off, while across the parking lot, a long line was forming at every porta-potty. The crewboss ordered everyone up and advised that "if you needed to shit, get in a porta-potty line, and if you just have to pee, don't tie up a porta-potty." The sight of masses of young men peeing in every available bush was surreal. I noticed that the very few women among the ranks of firefighters were permitted to use the toilets in the headquarters building. After relieving ourselves and getting packed up, we were back in line for another sleeve of sandwiches, all the candy we could carry, and finally a stop to the water buffalo to refill canteens. Then we loaded onto a school bus where we discovered we'd be headed to a big fire on the Kootenai NF.

We drove and drove, all day long on the bus, with no air conditioning and metal-rimmed plastic seats, desperately trying to sleep. After dark, we pulled off the highway into a large fire camp where we were greeted again, with stadium lights illuminating every particle of dust in the air and millions of moths. I had never seen a fire camp before in the daylight, much less completely artificially illuminated. It seemed a strange, confusing and disorganized mass of tents, generators, stadium lights, and hundreds of firefighters milling around like they knew where they were going.

The boss went off to get a briefing, and I scrunched down in my plastic seat. I awoke to the boss talking to the driver and showing him a map. He then announced that since we were a "fresh crew," we would head right out to the fireline and take over from another crew holding a stretch of line.

The driver shut the door, and we bounced around for the next couple of hours on dusty switchback-filled dirt roads in the most complete darkness I'd ever known. Finally, we stopped at the designated point and piled out of the bus. The boss instructed us to fill up the canteens, grab a lunch, a tool, a coat, and a fire shelter. Our gear bags would be taken back to camp. Soon, a firefighter met us in a pick-up truck and briefed the boss on our assignment. All of us were exhausted except the crewboss, evidently. We then hiked along a trail for an hour or so with several folks trying to share the light of others' headlamps for fear of running out of battery. The smoke started to get thick, and I remember being alert to the excitement of fighting a 'campaign fire.' The smoke grew thicker as we hiked, and the crew we were replacing started passing us, as they went back down the trail. They were filthy like they had been out for weeks camping in soot and dirt. There were no conversations to be had, just "heys."

As we got up to the edge of the fire, I could see a massive hillside of glowing orange logs and stumps in a sparse stand of enormous fir trees; it was beautiful. The boss told us to spread out about a chain apart, and if anything sparked over the line, we were to put it out. Occasionally a tree would torch, but the fountain of embers never crossed our line. Ten or twenty other crews came up, while additional crews headed down. After a few hours, all the crew shuffling had ended and we were just there, almost alone, to hold our portion. The tree torching had subsided, and the warmth of the glowing landscape was welcome. I wanted so badly, as most others did as well, to lay down in the line and take a nap. But the boss warned that anyone who laid down would have their pay docked for the day. He stalked the line checking on everyone periodically just to be sure. I couldn't understand how he had so much energy.

I squatted down and leaned onto my shovel handle, quickly learning that two legs and a shovel formed a pretty stable tripod. As I was dozing off the boss came by, checking to make sure no one was lying down. I wasn't. I felt like it was okay to sleep, just not lay down.

At some point in the night, I was abruptly knocked off my tripod by what felt like a baseball bat swung by a furious man. I tumbled and yelled in intense pain and confusion. My first thought was that the crewboss must have found me asleep and took a swing at me with his shovel. I squinted up toward the direction of some noise and saw a horse running down the fireline. Making sense of everything, it now seemed obvious that a horse had escaped from some nearby farm. Surely, it was panicked by the fire and running for its life when it plowed right into me. How weird!

The crewboss barked at me, "you okay?!" Some others from my crew who had circled around me were asking the same thing. I stood up with no apparent broken bones and asked the onlookers, *where the hell did that fuckin' horse come from?!* The crewboss laughed and said, "you must have been asleep because that wasn't no fuckin' horse, that was a fuckin' moose!"

That night and for the rest of the three-week assignment my name was changed from Steve to Bullwinkle.

Uncooked Poultry

Story by: Rikki Luebke

It was the first day of my first off-forest assignment and I was the rookie on the engine. We were assigned to Division Foxtrot on the Tucker fire, Modoc National Forest. Even though our task was to mop-up a mostly dead desert fire I could hardly contain my excitement. It was another busy fire season in California, but it had been a pretty slow start for my engine.

As we were combing the desert looking for hot spots, one of the seasonals came across a dead bird. The feathers were singed and the bird had been flash cooked in a fast-moving desert fire. He looked at the other seasonal and said "I'll give you $100 to take a bite out of this bird." The other seasonal quickly replied, "fuck, no." He then turned to me and offered $200, thinking the only girl on the engine would never be interested in that bet. I started thinking about it, but not too long because he started counting down from 10 at which the offer would no longer be on the table. I grabbed the bird from his hands confirming the bet. I gave the bird a quick inspection and decided to bite into its back, where it appeared to be the most cooked.

The creator of the bet started to take a video as I tore into the bird, chewing and then dramatically spitting the uncooked pink chunk onto the ground while the guys roared with laughter. I immediately ran back to the engine and brushed my teeth multiple times desperately trying to get the taste of uncooked grouse and burnt feathers out of my mouth! I rummaged through my sack lunch and discovered a Jolly Rancher, which I found worked well for covering up the horrible taste in my mouth. I managed to coax all the guys into giving me their Jolly Ranchers and proceeded to binge on them for the remainder of the shift. When my captain found out what happened, I quickly earned the nickname Ozzy. So, it was only fitting that we listened to some Ozzy Osbourne as we rolled back to camp that night.

"Captain's View" Watercolor
by Tonja Opperman

THE BISON AND THE WILDFIRE

Poem by: Paul Keller

Black Hills Fire, South Dakota

I watch the smoke and tiny stars of flame,
The night opening behind us in wind-drunk fire
Inside the huge red moons of your eyes.

How could I have known as I flagged this route out
That you were waiting here for the sound of my bones?
One thousand years of blood and dust and dung.

Now, inside your ears, my crew's first voices. A horrible
chant of power saws and hand tools. Their slow attack
echoes toward us. So I promise to stay with you all night,

To whisper into this radio cinched against my heart,
To warn them if you should turn and spin your great weight
Past sumac and chokecherry into the sound of their lives.

Above us, inside the black sky on those old Sioux ridges,
Shapes of white pine begin to remember themselves
Back into flame. Your giant skull heaves up

Into such a terrible silence. The dry peppery taste
Of skunkbush heating your breath, this night, the fire,
Your ancient passion to kill me. I move even closer.

You are the biggest animal I have ever dreamed.
Will either of us ever understand this fragile hate
Rising between us? I hear myself speak to you.

Tomorrow I will tell them everything. How you
Warned me like thunder with sudden low grunts.
How, even so, I followed you back into your dark.

Into this crazy bison and wildfire true story.
I was so young and fell in love with this danger.
With your eyes. With your sweet skunkbush breath.

Having a Bit of a Fitbit

Storytellers: Wally Ochoa and Bre Orcasitas

Bre:
Alright, Wall, you start. Tell me what you remember.

Wall:
Okay, what I remember is we were mopping up, but I can't remember exactly where it was. Somewhere in Washington...I know it was in Washington. And fire camp was there at that fish hatchery, right?

Bre:
Yep.

Wall:
We were pretty stuck on that one piece of ground for about three, four days at least, if not more. And it was mostly dead. And I remember my Fitbit was on me, you know, so that I could see what my heart rate was and everything well,

Bre:
And this was 2014 right? Yeah, yeah. It was.

Wall:
Was it earlier?

Bre:
That was the year I was on the heat stress module, and I was tied in with you guys for that. It was the season I was pregnant, so it had to be 2014.

Wall:
Oh, dang really? The year of my accident?*

Bre:
Yeah. It was only about a month before your accident. Wait, why did I bring up what year it was? Oh, oh... I remember. Because that Fitbit you had was one of the original versions. It wasn't like a watch the way they are now.

Wall:
Yeah, it was just a little bitty thing.

Bre:
Yeah, it looked a lot like one of those things that people used to stick in their ear to talk on the phone. You know? One of the early version 'hands-free' things. And wasn't your Fitbit dark gray in color?

Wall:

It was a black one I thought. Gray or black? Oh, I can't remember, but it was a dark color.

Bre:

And where did you keep it, in your shirt pocket? Is that where you had it when you lost it?

Wall:

Yeah, I would keep it in my shirt pocket and it must have fallen out when I was bent over mopping up. We were mopping up for a while and gosh, at some point I noticed it was gone. So, I went back trying to retrace my steps where I was and stuff because our area was so dead. I had plenty of time to look for it.

Bre:

Yeah, like you said it was so dead and mop-up was kind of slow and boring, a bunch of us started to help you look. And we looked for a while. I mean, how long do you think we looked for that thing?

Wall:

All-day almost.

Bre:

I can picture that area too. It was just typical fire ground, you know? The fire had gone through and everything was burned over and there were just these tiny little bits of burnt twigs and stuff all over the ground. And I thought, Yeah, this is like finding a needle in a needle stack. Because the color and size of your Fitbit looked like everything else on the ground, ha!

Wall:

Yeah. And then I started looking at the app on my phone remember? Because the app tracked it. And that's when it was saying it was over there by the tree and so we went over there.

Bre:

We looked and looked all around there. But nothin'. And you kept saying, "It should be right here. It keeps saying that it's right here. It's nearby that tree."

Wall:

And then it started telling us it was in a different spot... over there a ways. The tracker was putting it in different spots and at one point we joked like oh, some friggin' animal's probably running around with it and messing with us!

Bre:

Ha! Yeah. Eventually, we kind of gave up because we couldn't figure out what the hell was going on with it. A technology glitch or something. And it was like mission impossible to find that thing anyway.

Wall:

Uh-huh. We looked for so long too! That's when that gentleman came up. Who was he?

Bre:

He was someone on the heat stress module with me.

Wall:

Oh, yeah.

Bre:

He handed you the Fitbit and you're like, what?! Where? And he said he was just sitting down grabbing a bite when a chipmunk. Or squirrel? Which one was it?

Wall:

Oh, I can't remember now. It was some sort of furry little creature.

Bre:

I think maybe a chipmunk? Anyhow, the thing came up right in front of him with the friggin' Fitbit in its mouth! Did he drop it in front of him like a dog does with a ball? What happened?

Wall:

I think he had it in his mouth but then got startled and dropped it.

Bre:

Yeah. That sounds right. So, then he walks up to us and re-member? He was like, "You are never going to believe what just happened... I was just sitting down to eat my lunch when this chipmunk scurried up and dropped off your Fit-bit. Haven't you been looking for this for like three hours?"

Wall:

[Laughter] It really was an animal messin' with us that whole time!

Bre:

Probably bouncin' right over our heads in the branches of that tree, ha! That chipmunk was one hell of a prankster, [Laughter]

Wall:

[Laughter] It sure was. And it just kept that thing in its mouth for hours! Running around with it like that. Messin' with us.

Bre:

I still can't believe that happened.

Wall:

Me either.

*Wally Ochoa is the survivor of the Freezeout Ridge incident of 2014.

If You Give a Mouse a Chance

Story by: Betty

We were assigned to a fire in Oregon in September of 2009. Already late in the season, we were starting to see hints of Snaptember, which were only exacerbated by our daily assignments. We had for several days been breaking down windrows built on the wrong side of an indirect line, daisy-chaining giant rounds to the correct side. We had also built a lot of indirect hand line which was later deemed unnecessary as strategies for managing the fire changed. Fast-forward a few miserable days, which were made survivable by the camaraderie of our close-knit crew, and we finally received a good operational assignment. We would be burning out along a road to tidy up one side of the fire.

So, we headed out to the line and crew assignments were made. I was assigned to holding and we headed out to line the dirt road. As the lighters got closer to where I was standing, one of them noticed a tiny mouse frantically trying to stay ahead of the flames they were laying down. The mouse flitted out onto the road, desperate to get away from the fire, but it was scared back into the black when it saw one of our holders in between it and the green. The mouse quickly tried to make another escape but was again too afraid to forge on past our holders. At this point, all of our igniters and nearby holders were cheering the little mouse on with each attempt it made. We wanted it to run to safety, but we kept scaring it and the mouse appeared to be getting tired.

Collectively, we came up with a plan: Our squad boss would use his rhino to flick the mouse onto the road, hoping to get it going in the right direction. While he did that, those of us nearby would stand completely still, giving the mouse no reason to retreat.

The plan was initiated. Our squad boss found the mouse and gently launched it onto the dirt road. We all stood completely still, barely moving our heads as we watched the mouse tentatively make its way towards the green. It was working! Everyone was excited; the anticipation was building. Would the mouse make it?

As our squad's designated photographer, I took my camera out to film this momentous event. But then, the mouse stopped, seemingly contemplating its next move. The mouse began to move again, still headed towards the green, but it had changed its course slightly; the mouse was now moving in my direction. But I held firm, I had agreed to not move!

The mouse continued to edge closer to me when suddenly -at lightning speed- the mouse raced toward the toe of my boot, scurrying past my ankle and right into my pant leg, passing the top of my 14-inch boot, and making it all the way to my knee before my frantic Hokey Pokey moves (you put your right leg in...) knocked it loose from its precarious climb up my leg and back on its route to the green.

While it felt like an eternity, I know that the entire event took less than a few seconds...I have evidence... yes, I had been filming it, and you can hear every unintelligible noise that came out of my mouth as the camera shook while I desperately tried to eject the small mouse from its unfortunate foray up the pantleg of a firefighter.

Oh, and if you're still wondering... the mouse made it safely into the green.

"Flare-up on the Fireline" Watercolor
by Tonja Opperman

Bear Tango

Story by: Tony Allabastro

The year was 2008. It was my rookie season on a hotshot crew. We were assigned to the Lehardy fire in Yellowstone National Park and our crew was operating in Hayden valley, which is apparently the "bear mecca" of the park with around 130 bears residing in that valley. We had been seeing a few each day since we began work there without any incident. On this day we were in the middle of a large-scale L-pattern backfire, tying into the Yellowstone River to create a catcher's mitt for the fire to burn into. This patch of forest was one of the unhealthiest I had ever been in; with head height and above of jackstraw dead-and-down to fight our way through. We had five lighters with 50-foot spacing and we could barely see each other through all the deadfall. So, we were making lots of noise, singing and hooting and hollering so we could keep tabs on each other and keep our line straight.

I was the last lighter in line furthest from the green. It was several hours into the burn, and we were starting to close in on the river. I was walking on top of some downed logs, dropping a dot of fire every 30 feet or so. That's when I heard some branches break to my left. I looked up to see a Grizzly bear standing about 50 feet in front of me. I hopped off the logs and started walking in the opposite direction, trying to slip back into the brush. I took a few steps and looked over my shoulder to see where the bear was, only to find that it was in a full charge, crashing through the brush, and coming straight at me.

I remember looking down at my torch thinking, "Maybe I could set it on fire?" I had heard rumors that if you hit a bear on the nose, they tear up kind of like a shark; "Maybe I could use my tool and hit it on the nose?" Then before I realized it, I started running. At best, I made it 9 feet before the bear closed the gap and took me to the ground. I don't remember too many specifics of what the bear did because frankly, I didn't want to look at it. However, I distinctly remember feeling the immense weight of the bear and its sheer power as it tossed me around like a plastic bag.

At one point, I heard a high-pitched scream like it came from a third grader and then realized that it was actually coming out of me! A feeling of embarrassment swept over me and I'm sure I turned beet red. For a split second all I could think was, "Really? This is how you're handling this? This is how you're going to go out? " That moment ended up being a good turning point because I decided that rather than just take the beating, I was going to do something to get myself out of it. I was able to crawl into a pile of logs so that my torso was covered but left my legs exposed. Just past my feet the bear was standing, swaying from side-to-side, and watching me. By this point, the rest of the crew had realized what was happening and my radio was blowing up, which was not optimal for my current circumstance with the bear. My hands were shaking from all the adrenaline, and I was having a hard time turning the tiny volume knob off on my radio. So, I began punching it, trying to silence it manually. The next thing I knew, the bear pulled me back out into the open and crawled on top of me. With its hind legs standing on the backs of my thighs, it stood up then punched down on my shoulder blades with its front legs, knocking all the wind out of me. The upside was it was easier to be quiet with no air in my lungs. The bear did that move on me twice then began to paw at me. It would swat at me, then waited a second, and then pawed some more. I wrapped my arms around my head and held it tightly into the dirt. Then all of a sudden, I felt the weight lift off of me. I didn't turn around to look because I was convinced the bear was still just a few steps away. After a bit, I slowly turned my head to find that it had run off.

One of the first people to make it to me after the bear had left was a squad leader who later said I was muttering and overturning logs searching for my helmet when he got to me. He had me sit down and then, hot on his heels, came one of our EMTs. He did a quick head-to-toe check on me and informed me all my major organs were thankfully on the inside where they belonged, but there was a lot of blood making it look worse. He asked if I could walk, and I said yes, to which he replied, "Good because it's time to go." All the dots of fire we had put on the ground were beginning to come together and the fire intensity was picking up. With isolated group tree torching flaring up around us, we half-walked/half-ran about a mile out to a meadow where they landed a helicopter to medivac me to the park hospital. A second helicopter was launched simultaneously with park rangers and a gunner to track the bear and see if it was aggressive or a threat. They said the bear was a three-year-old male that stood about 10 feet tall on its hind legs. The rangers determined that he was probably scared by the fire and trying to escape, which prompted his aggression toward me. Once he felt the threat was mitigated (i.e. me) he moved on. They opted to not put him down, which I felt was appropriate.

My saving grace in the whole encounter was that the bear never bit me. Instead, he bit the top pouch of my fire pack and a full MSR canister of chainsaw fuel crushing it down to under an inch. I'm pretty sure that the mouthful of gas

was a big deterrent and ended up helping my overall out-
come. All said and done I received claw marks to the back
of the head, neck, shoulders, and thighs; jet-black bruising
from my knees to my hips, a few broken ribs, and three
claw marks that went right through the crew emblem on
my helmet. I commend my fellow crewmembers for their
quick and decisive actions, what they did directly contrib-
uted to my smooth and efficient extrication. Above all else,
I'm grateful that I ended up with nothing more than some
minor injuries and a good story to tell around the campfire.

CHAPTER 3
THAT JUST HAPPENED

"The Incredible Floating Cubee" Chalk and Sharpie
By Anonymous

Haiku
by: Lookout Laura

morning pika song

hauling cubees, one by
one

our hearts are muscles

Vienna Sausages

Story by: Milly

No shit, there I was sitting at helibase in Northern California. It was day 4, 6, 8, I don't remember for sure, all I know is that we'd been there a while hooking/unhooking buckets and "available for IA." It was late afternoon when a radio transmission came from dispatch sending us to a new start. After punching in the coordinates, we figured out it was in a pretty remote area. Odd place for a new start when it had been at least a week since the last lightning bust. Must be a holdover.

Six of us rappelled the fire and were first on scene with six jumpers en route. We started putting line in at the heel of the fire, and after a few minutes I walked ahead to scout the line and do some hot shoveling. The first thing I noticed that was out of the ordinary were wads of toilet paper; someone had surface shit here recently. That's strange, we just got here. And none of us would commit such an act. I kept walking and the next thing I found was irrigation tubing. I got on the radio and called the IC to let him know my findings. Right around the same time period, our spotter (who had been dropped off on a high point nearby) had just hooked the bucket to the helicopter and called us on the radio to say, "Hey, I just saw 6 guys in fatigues run by me." It was becoming very apparent that we had just rappelled into a marijuana grow operation.

The jumpers arrived, and the 12 of us kept digging line and working with the aircraft to contain the fire. On my way up the right flank I came across the plants, some makeshift structures with marijuana drying in them, and what appeared to be the farmers' mess tent. The LEOs (law enforcement officers) were called, and they were making their way to the fire from the bottom. They radioed to inform us that the whole drainage was planted and that it was most likely a cartel operation. The LEOs decided they had seen enough and were turning back. They advised us to not spend the night.

The problem with bailing off the fire was that we had not yet evaluated an extraction point, and we had seen from the flight in that there were cliff bands below us. We had about a half hour of light left and hiking down in the dark, navigating cliff bands, through a marijuana grow, with 6 strangers dressed in fatigues sharing the same hillside as us, was not a good option. We were spending the night.

As it grew dark, we walked out into the green off the left

flank of the fire and into a thick brushy area where we hunkered down for the night; no warming fire, no headlamps, and radios turned way down. For dinner I reached into our food bag and pulled a can out in the dark. I got into my sleeping bag -which turns out I deployed in or near an ant pile- and opened my mystery can, ready for dinner. The can I had chosen was vienna sausages. As I enjoyed my cold, slippery, gelatinous can of sausages with the ants that had now started to invade my sleeping bag (they weren't biting ants so that was a win), in the dark, we heard the fatigue dressed farmers off in the distance, not sure what they were up to. Maybe they came back for their belongings before they had to leave this place? That's what I told myself anyway as I went to sleep.

The next morning, we smashed some visible smokes on the fire and headed for the LZ (landing zone) that was picked out for us at the top of the mountain. We were extracted from the fire by late morning.

From that point on, every time I see a can of vienna sausages it takes me back to the night on the hillside we spent with the ants, the weed plants, the surface shit, and the fatigue dressed cartel pot farmers.

Typical Night Shift

Story by: Downtown Sarah Brown

Allow me to me set the stage. It was late in the season of 2009. There wasn't much going on in the rappel world so, when a large fire broke out in southern Oregon, three of us region 6 rappel crews patched together a 20-person hand crew. The dynamics of the crew were interesting, to say the least. We had a crew boss and crew boss trainee naturally, but aside from that, we had about six qualified crew bosses on the crew. All but two were IC5s, and every crew member was at least a qualified squad boss. If you know anything about rappellers, you know that they usually manage themselves just fine. For a crew boss trainee, this had potential to be a worst-case scenario; herding a group of independent/overqualified cats. And on night shift, nonetheless.

My story begins on a forest road somewhere, with fire burning on one side and not the other. It was our first night there, and it wasn't very exciting. The fire was smoldering and calm. So, we spent the first part of our shift walking up and down the road looking for any spot fires across the road, or hazard trees that might come down. The crewboss had put together a saw squad who were tasked with driving up and down the road looking for hazard trees as well.

As the night drew on, there was less and less activity as the temperature dropped. We congregated into small groups in the wee hours of the morning to huddle around small, warming fires as we took turns walking up and down the road. Things were still pretty quiet. On occasion, the saw squad would drive by patrolling the road, but that was about it. Just a typical night shift.

The night was wearing on and we all started getting the nods. Four of us were hunkered around the campfire when we saw the rig carrying the saw squad coming slowly down the road. It was a huge truck with a "box" on the back for storing helicopter equipment. We called it the ice cream truck and it was easy to spot. This time when the truck rolled up, it stopped. The driver shouted "Hey!" then killed the lights, cranked the knob on the stereo way up, and began blasting rave music into the night. Suddenly, four squad members burst open the back doors and jumped out decorated with glow sticks, they began rave dancing to the music. They had also attached glow sticks to strings and sticks that they wildly swung, twirled, and launched into the air. The four of us just sat there wide-eyed in silence as we watched them gyrate and techno dance in the dead of night. It was magical.

Then, just as abruptly as it began, the music stopped. The driver yelled, "load up!" and the saw squad jumped back into the box, closed the door, and slowly headed down the road leaving us in dark and silence once again.

"Aerial Recon" Watercolor
by Tonja Opperman

Comin' in HOT!

Story by: Jumper 1

The alarm sounded and I was one of the four rappellers on the ready load. We all scrambled to use our precious few minutes wisely before running out to the ready shack to gear up. For me, the siren is like a starting gun for a one-person race to the bathroom. I'd learned from experience that the next bathroom opportunity is always fleeting when aircraft is involved.

After gearing-up, and stuffing whatever goodies we could into our flight suits, we moved with purpose out to the spooled-up aircraft. From there we fell into the choreography of procedures that have been relentlessly drilled into every rappeller since rookie training. Check your own self, do a buddy check with someone, get your spotter check, and check the spotter. Then you advance to entering the aircraft, for a check of the rappel equipment. Once the spotter takes their seat and double checks that we've all done our checks, the spotter double checks our safety harnesses and the equipment before we can finally depart. Amazingly, somehow all of that can happen within the neighborhood of five minutes.

Spooled and ready, the helicopter bounced in anticipation until finally, we lifted from the ground. Of course, by then all of us were hot and sweaty from being layered up in our rappel gear and having to cram together on an inhospitable bench seat. Fortunately, it wasn't too long in transit before we arrived at our little fire.

As is customary, the helicopter circled several times so that everyone on board could do a good size-up of the fire. Another order of business while still in the air was to evaluate escape routes, potential safety zones, and a viable packout route. Once all that had been accomplished the four of us unplugged our comms to prepare for rappel ops, the rest of our communication would rely solely on hand signals.

Rappel ops was another choreographed dance pulled up from the memory of all parties involved. Every rappeller goes through rookie rappel academy and that training includes an insane amount of repetition mixed with small graduated steps. First is ground training, then advancement to the low tower, and eventually quality time spent dangling from the high tower. After high tower come mock-ups until finally, you go live. First rappelling from 50 feet, then progressing in height each time until reaching, 250 feet, the height of a standard operational rappel. A height at which a 75 foot tall tree looks like a shrub.

While rookie rappellers are single-mindedly focused on retaining lifesaving procedures during rappel academy, they are simultaneously given a laundry list of do and don't protocols by the trainers to shove into their brains as well. Successfully navigating rookie training and annual recertifications is what ultimately led this load of rappellers to be rappelling from a helicopter into a wildfire.

The spotter slid the doors open, allowing a much welcome burst of air into the fuselage. After talking the pilot into the rappel spot over the radio, the helicopter was set in a hover and ready to lighten its load. The spotter dropped ropes and turned to the first stick of rappellers, giving the "unbuckle" signal. The next signal told us to exit the aircraft (one rappeller exits out each side) and steady ourselves in a wide stance on the skids of the helicopter. Sometimes the aircraft drifts, which prompts dialogue between the spotter and pilot to get the helicopter repositioned. In times like these, rappellers are quite literally left to hang out on the skid, and these moments are always my least favorite. It gives me too much time to think about what I'm doing, or just how many things could go wrong. As I stared up at all the moving parts of the rotor spinning overhead, I just wanted to get my signal already. Then finally, it came, and down we went.

Once rappellers hit the ground, the protocol is to unhook from the descent device and clear the rappel spot immediately. It helps the spotter to get eyes on the rappellers so that they know it's clear either for a second stick or for cargo letdown (rappeller cargo consists of a fire box and saw box, which contain all the equipment needed to fight fire); but it's also a safety measure. Our second stick came sliding down, and shortly after they cleared the rappel spot, over the deafening rotor wash, I heard and felt, a BOOM!

I swung around to see that a saw box had apparently gotten away from the spotter and augered itself into the ground. After the spotter finished letting down the other cargo boxes and the helicopter peeled away, we all raced over to assess the damage. We flung off the cargo harness and cracked open the box to witness a horrific spectacle. A brand-spankin' new Stihl 440 smashed to bits. *I understand if you need to take a moment of silence here before continuing on.* As if that weren't bad enough, we actually needed a saw on this fire so the spotter had to let down a second saw box. On the face of it, that doesn't sound like a big deal except that it is a BIG deal. Here's why: Everything that gets lowered to the ground comes out of the forest on your back. After a fire is out, rappellers (and jumpers as well) pack all their fire gear/supplies into large packout bags, then bushwhack across the formidable landscape for several miles before reaching a feasible pick-up point. A standard pack-out bag weighs between 85-110 lbs, and each person gets one, yay! Which means, we were just gifted an additional 60 lbs to pack out on our backs.

Another fun component to our circumstance was that adverse weather was set to move in the following day and we were on very steep terrain, the last thing we needed was slick ground with heavy weight. After having a look at the fire, we determined that our best course of action was for two people to work the fire, while the other two packed out all the broken and/or unnecessary gear to stage at our pick-up point. I ended up in the packout twosome. We quickly planned our route, packed up, and began the slow slog down the mountain to stage our gear.

As we began, I noticed that the slope was coated in dead needle cast, which made the ground really slick. On more than one occasion my feet came out from under me before I even had a chance to react. Falling with that much weight on your back is a bit of an art form because the potential for injury is so high. You can't hold your arms out to brace yourself without potentially snapping your wrist or hyper-extending an elbow. You've just got to let the bag take you where it wants to go, and hope you can break yourself free from it if you start picking up momentum.

Eventually, we made it to the bottom. *Well,* near the bottom might be more accurate. With the dirt road in sight, we had gotten cliffed-out. It wasn't that far down to the road, maybe 20 ft? But we ultimately decided to stow our bags up above and figure the rest out later. There was nothing left to do but hike back up the steep, steep slope. On the upside, we didn't have any weight on our backs, so that's something.

Amazingly, this little mission took most of the day and had us getting back to camp at dusk. Just in time to crack open my food box and make some dinner. The fire itself was all but out by the time we made it back, so all four of us took it easy. Feeling a bit haggard from packout #1, I was happy to sit around the cooking fire trying to perfect my spicy V8 marinated spam recipe.

The next morning as is customary, we got down on hands and knees to feel around with our bare hands for heat before beginning the 6-hour watch. What's a 6-hour watch? Essentially, you hang out with the fire, and if a smoke pops up within the 6-hour stretch, you start the clock all over again. The 6-hour watch can easily be handled by one person, which frees everyone else up to break down camp, fill out paperwork, and pack up the beloved packout bags. With the storm looming out in the distance, we were able to bomb down the hill before it reached us; that last 20 feet was a bit tricky though. We managed to use the cargo letdown lines to lower our packout bags, and then we used them on ourselves to rappel down to the road.

After returning to the base we unpacked our packout bags, refurbed the gear, and took stock of the busted-up saw. Some parts could be salvaged, but mostly it was totaled. Assuming the spotter was feeling a little sheepish about exploding a brand-new saw, I figured he deserved a little pick-me-up. I grabbed broken components from the saw and created a mobile that I sneakily hung over his desk. That way, when he looked up, it would appear as if the saw box was "comin' in hot!" As he walked into his office, several of us were there waiting for him. We presented the mobile with "Free Fallin' " by Tom Petty playing in the background because nothing cures what ails ya' more than laughter.

June 27th- The Day of the Fox

Story by: TM

Please Note: This story focuses on the loss of a parent and may be triggering to some who have had similar experiences. However, this story is very relatable to those who've found themselves receiving bad news while on the fireline surrounded by fire family.

June 27th, 2011; I remember that day vividly. We were on the Monument fire just south of Sierra Vista, Arizona and my shot crew was spiked out on a ridgetop where I could gaze through the smoke, right down into Mexico. That morning I awoke to the most incredible sunrise; rich, velvety reds and watercolor translucent purples brushed the sky. We were preparing to leave our spike camp that day and head down to get another assignment elsewhere on the fire. After everyone had packaged up the gear to sling it out, we got into formation to grid for micro trash. A crew ritual before leaving each spike camp, I lined out next to a close buddy who always had my six. We had only moved about 20 paces when I felt the vibration in my pocket – my phone. Instantly my body trembled, and I felt sick. Deep in my soul, I knew what this call was.

You see, just a couple of months prior we found out that my mother had terminal cancer. It was an aggressive, ruthless, violent cancer. It had embedded itself into her brain, lungs, and lymphatic system. She was at home living out her last days in the sunroom that she and my dad had built 25 years earlier. He had ripped the logs (wood beams) with a mill and his chainsaw, and my mom had sanded them by hand.

Between this assignment and our previous one in Alaska, I had rushed home to spend 30 precious hours with her; cherishing every minute that I had the ability to hold her fragile hand. We listened to music together and I sat with a tight, gnawing feeling anchored in the back of my throat, fighting against the urge to weep while John Prine's song "Paradise" filled the air around us.

Now, on this day in June, that tight gnawing feeling had returned to my throat as I opened my phone and held it to my ear. The world stood still. My crew turned and looked at me as I answered and heard the words uttered by my dad, "Mom has moved onto another realm..." I instantly fell to my knees and sobbed. My buddy knelt down beside me and gently placed his hand on my back. My squad boss handed me a white crystal she had in her pocket. My superintendent got on the phone to orchestrate a swift demob.

That night, I walked into the baggage claim area of my hometown met by my husband, (also a hotshot) who had navigated his own challenging set of logistics to be here with me in this moment. We embraced, and I inhaled the smoke and salty sweat aroma on his crew shirt. It felt strangely comforting. On June 27th, I lost my mother and part of my identity. She was my adoptive mother who swooped me up in her arms when I was just three months old and cherished me as blood.

On the two-year anniversary of my mom's passing, our crew was spiked out on a ridgeline in Colorado, breathing in the thin mountain air at 9,000 ft elevation. The night was crisp and the stars were vibrant white dots hanging overhead. I had laid out my sleeping bag on my tarp, situated my PG bag to act as a pillow, and snuggled in. Later in the night I was awoken by something walking on my tarp, just above my head. I turned in my sleeping bag to see a red fox batting the straps of my PG bag.

Some believe in spirits that inhabit this world; those seeking closure before moving on to another realm. Until that moment, I had struggled painfully to process my mom's passing and had yearned for one last connection. I would desperately try to find meaning in a random bird sighting, an obscure flower or a shadow cast on the wall. But this quiet night gifted me a moment of healing I will forever cherish.

The fox's gaze met mine as she cocked her head to the side, and the world stopped for a moment as I gently whispered; "Hi, Mom." At last, I could say hello and goodbye in one breath. That sweet and gentle interaction on the crisp night of June 27th was a fleeting, curious blessing. And as I turned around onto my back to face the stars once again, a tear rolled down my cheek.

"Winter Forest" Charcoal from an Arizona Wildfire
Size: 11 x 14"
By Stephanie Peters

CHAPTER 4
PONDERINGS

"Wall of Flame" Watercolor

By Tonja Opperman

We Celebrate Gorgeous

Poem by: Emma Ruth Anderson

You still
bleed blue, baby
from a one hour fuel.
Chainsaws, hand tools,
and twenty-odd people
came together to make a crew.
Dedicated to celebrate, appreciate
a slow season for what it was:
an opportunity to learn, (if nothing else but patience,
goodness gracious). Fire found us family and
these lights will always burn.

The Unforgettables

Story by: AP

Countless moments have gone by to get us to where we are now. While most of those moments were passed through without even a second thought, some vaguely linger in our awareness unwittingly instilling an imprint in who we are. Some moments can be so defining that your entire mentality shifts in the blink of an eye. The latter are what I like to call the "unforgettables."

Unforgettable moments aren't solely confined to work in this job; everyone has their defining moments that got them to where they are, but many of my most profound *unforgettables* came from experiences I've had in fire. There are certain things I'll never forget, like my first season on the hotshot crew in 2009 when we had our first "real" hotshot roll. We had been assigned to the Backbone fire in the devilishly beautiful and intimidating Shasta-Trinity National Forest. After getting flown to the remote backcountry, our first task was to hike down (a long way down) from a helispot, "H-19", to our division. I spent the majority of that hike focused on not making any missteps as we continued descending further and further down. I remember the relief

I felt after having successfully made it to the end without tripping into my saw partner, or dropping the dolmar of fuel that I had been balancing over my shoulder with the business end of my tool. However, that feeling of relief quickly transitioned into work mode, as I spent my first day as a freshly designated swamper learning through failure and observation. I watched in awe of the other saw teams who'd been working together for years; communicating through non-verbals without missing a beat, and hoping that someday I could get to that level.

It didn't cross my mind until the end of the shift that we also had to hike back UP that steep, steep, mountain. I don't recall how far it was, or how long it took, but I do recall the burning sensation in my legs while trying to quiet that little inner voice telling me, "Just step off to the side and grab a quick break." But I knew I couldn't stop because 19 other people were hiking the same nasty piece of ground with me. Whether they were feeling more, less, or the same amount of pain didn't matter. What mattered was that we were all suffering together, and somehow that gave me just enough motivation to keep going until we reached the top. That hike helped me to recognize the power of the crew dynamic -we weren't going to let each other down- and I could feel an unshakable sense of accountability and camaraderie building within me from that point on.

The more I thought about it, I began to realize that all the unforgettable memories I have tucked away in my mind had more to do with the people than the experience or environment itself, people were the common denominator. This is not to say that all my unforgettables are the friend-liest of memories. There have been times where I've gotten into some drawn out, dig your heels in, uncomfortable, we're hashing this drama out right now, type situations with people that I highly respect. And then there were other times, like when my superintendent humbled me by saying, "sometimes it is your fault," when I was passing the buck instead of owning my actions. It was hard to hear at the time but truly valued.

Of course, there are funny unforgettables that always stick out the most. One fire season my best friend (and fellow crewmember) found a traffic cone and started carrying it around with him. He would sneak up behind people, move the cone near their ear, and then make a loud sound, scaring the crap out of them; it worked every time. One day he pulled his cone move on a sleeping crewmember in the back of the buggy and the guy's reaction as he awoke from a dead sleep was so funny that everyone in the buggy almost peed their pants laughing!

There are also the straight-to-the-core ones. One set of un-

forgettables was seeing my dad lead by example throughout the years that we worked together on the hotshot crew.
Up until then, I had only gotten to hear stories from his
fellow crewmembers about his incredible work ethic, the
positive attitude he carried himself with, and the amazing things people had seen him do. He was someone the
entire crew looked up to throughout his many years on the
hotshot crew. His final fire season, we were both sawyers
on separate saw teams; he was obviously 1st saw and that
most definitely wasn't up for debate! Getting that opportunity to work with him over those years was truly special.
Seeing all those moments firsthand, that would later turn
into stories shared by the crew; that was a blessing. Not
many people get to have the unique experience of working
on a hotshot crew with their dad, and I get to carry those
memories with me.

Unforgettable people and memories throughout the years
have helped to shape my outlook on life, how I carry
myself, and how I respond to adversity. I appreciate them
all for who and what they are, and the mark they've left on
me. Sometimes I wonder, without the unforgettables who
would I be?

"Firing Operations" Watercolor
By Tonja Opperman

Perspective

Story by: Courtney McGee

My first season in fire was a wake-up call. I wasn't fully prepared for all of the physical and mental challenges that would come with the job, but looking back on it, can a rookie ever fully know what a fire job is going to be like? I struggled to keep up and had a lot of self-doubt about whether I was the right person for the job. Something that stood out in the beginning, was that there was much more yelling than what I was used to, which sort of frightened me at the time.

When we got our first fire assignment it was challenging but exciting, and a rush. We spent the first week on a hillside grass fire in Southern California that burned and went out really quickly. From there we were sent to the Soberanes fire on the Los Padres National Forest. We spent our days hiking steep ground and cutting line in a forest full of poison oak, it was everywhere and totally unavoidable; I had never seen anything like it.

I knew from past experience that I was susceptible to poison oak so I figured I'd get it, but I had no idea what I was in for. Over the next week a poison oak rash slowly spread over a solid 50% of my body. I ended up having to get the steroid shot but nothing really seemed to help. I somehow made it through to the end of the roll but I spent my R&R days suffering through the rash.

It ended up being so bad that when I went back to work I couldn't even get my boots on because my feet were so swollen. I walked up to my crew supt. in tears, explaining to him that I needed to go back to the doctor. He was sympathetic to my situation and had someone drive me. Meanwhile, the crew ended up getting an assignment and going to another fire before I had fully recovered. Even though I was in such a sorry state I still couldn't help but feel like I was letting the crew down.

Flash forward to the end of the season when I was pulled into the office for my end-of-season performance review. I was certain that all my shortcomings would be pointed out and I'd be asked not to come back for another season, but I was so wrong. Instead, the crew overhead proceeded to tell me that I displayed natural leadership amongst my peers and that they were looking forward to giving me more leadership opportunities the following season if I'd like to return. I happily accepted their offer and committed to two more seasons on the crew.

My crew supt. instilled his trust in me, which helped me to become a confident and competent leader while also teaching me a lot about patience, resilience, balance, and communication. And as it turns out, I actually came to appreciate the yelling and sternness of our crew assistant who regularly demonstrated strength, discipline, and how to take initiative at work. The crew created an accepting place for me to grow and discover my strengths and weaknesses; I was pushed beyond physical and emotional limits that I didn't think were possible, but I was able to do it because I had the support of my crew.

Some of my favorite fireline memories are of the days where we got our asses kicked on a fire or from running saw all day. Those days are my favorite because we struggled, but we all struggled together and no matter how hard things got, we still found ourselves laughing at the end of the day. I'm so glad I took the plunge and made that commitment to fight fire. I'll forever be grateful for those experiences and for the people who will always hold a special place in my heart.

\\ 2016 //

Last Day of the Rodeo

Poem by: Emma Ruth Anderson

First fire season took us to California -
tufa, tan oak, Mariposa and pine.
Where beetles took the cedars
that the drought has left behind.

We licked our plates of fried chicken and
never touched the handrail.
Locked up rigs, emptied Siggs, learned
the 'right' way to blouse boots,
and shout crew hoots.
We filled chainsaw tanks with leaky dolmars,
drank water and gatos by the gallon,
sank bare-backed hands into the ash
searching for heat.

Spiked out in the Black Rock Desert:
broken bootstraps bound with glass tape,
a popped plastic cubee water bladder
plugged with MRE gum,
packed extra weight up the hill

so someone else doesn't have to.

Fire boiled the ground duff,
spoke softly to the inversion.
We ate breakfast, lunch, and dinner;
cut Doug fir, sagebrush, juniper.

Fire waited for the winds to change
and charged us out of the east-west drainage.
Fire coddled the long night through,
our sweat-drenched yellows
steaming deliriously in that 2 AM daze.

Fired up -
we pull the power trigger and
keep on until the tie-in,
and then some.

"Rock-n-Roll Crown Fire" Watercolor
By Tonja Opperman

Stitches

Story by: Caleb Miller

I've got the perfect pair of greens. It's not one that I pulled from the cache or was sent home with me after raiding a Type 1 team's supply, either. No way—these are my greens.

I got them in Colorado, when a contractor I'd applied to asked me to supply my own greens, then drive seven hours overnight to pack test with him the next morning otherwise I wouldn't get the job. My girlfriend at the time agreed to go with me, despite her own time constraints with going back to college. She was even there to give me that first look of approval when I stepped out of the changing room wearing a piece of clothing that would change my life. And—although the girl's gone, and that job is too—I've had the greens with me ever since.

I've had these greens from the swamps of Florida up to the interior of Alaska. They've been on recons, lookouts, burnouts, mop-ups, line-digs, saw cuts, pre-po's and stagings. They've been broken in by that crisp Montana air, tore through the Arizona salt cedar, and tangled with mustang grape in Texas. These greens are so well-worn they move like silk over my thighs and fold like air over my knees.

They've got those deep pockets on both the front and rear, as well as two-long cargo pockets that easily fit a manifest book, a manpurse, or a belt weather kit. They're double-layered in the crotch and elastic in the waist, so I don't have to wear suspenders or a belt if I don't want to. The fly is a snap and the zipper is smooth, and, although the Velcro on the pockets is falling apart, I never lose e-tape or my radio. Even my lighter and knife stay in the hip pockets, unless I have the good fortune to kick up my feet on a hotel couch once in a blue moon. And, then: the pants only slowly release the objects through a distinct glide of fabric well-known to my nerves by now. Though these pants might be a patchwork of dye sublimation and fraught needlepoint—I reckon they are the most stylish and most user-friendly unity of form-and-function trousers a firefighter will ever get.

They're not mints, and they ain't those olive disco pants—no way. They're that dark, almost bluish-green, color that sub-alpine firs sometimes turn when grown in cooler altitudes. A green like this makes any crew tee look that much more impressive. Blue, black, orange—hell, even red on these doesn't seem to stoke the nightmarish faux-pas of Christmas in July.

When I wear these pants, I feel invincible. Whether it's during a store stop or hiking into spike camp: the way these pants breathe and take a laissez-faire attitude to any movement makes the wearer feel like he or she is performing in the Cirque-du-Soleil of land management. Every movement is awe-inspiring: every improbability likely. I like to think that Prometheus himself gifted humankind with these pants, and, maybe—deep down—these pants were the hope hidden inside Pandora's box.

Yet, as all things too shall pass, these pants' glory-days are long since behind them. They no longer let themselves be thrown against the flames like their cache-ready counterparts. These pants have been there and done that, and they are now strictly travel pants. They are for the day on which all uncertainties have been laid to rest, and the comforts of home are so close you can touch them. These pants say, "Job well-done," and, "You're in good hands now." So—as I thread another needle to once more sew the Velcro on the hem, I am reminded of the memories of good friendship and the moxie that they bring.

A Belt Digs

Poem by: Andrew Foster Armstrong

A belt digs
Into my hips, where my pack sits

My neck and shoulders tighten
Under the load I carry

My back screams a flame
Of searing pain

My ankles twist
From loose ground and heavy weight

My skin hurts
My feet, back, hands
Constant irritation

A drop of sweat roles
Down the same path as the previous
Sometimes one chooses its own path

But I'm alive

And I feel grateful
To be able to experience pain

People too often hide from the uncomfortable
Like it's a bad thing
To be uncomfortable

I disagree

So, skin blisters
Muscles ache
And a belt digs
I let it

"The Scout," Pyrography on Basswood Plaque
By Sheena Waters

Humility

Story by: Chris Surgenor

The air is stale and hot in the cramped passenger compartment of the airplane. Men and women with shoulders crowded in the claustrophobic innards of a CASA 212. It's an old cargo plane built by the Spaniards in the '80s. The guts have been torn out of her and wires run through the exposed aluminum ribs and ceiling of her interior. Naked metal benches painted aircraft gray are all that remain. The decor is... austere. Those in the rear are the lucky ones. Air circulates through the open side door, dispelling queasy stomachs and comforting frayed nerves.

It's August and the air wafting through the compartment is a mixture of drift smoke, Jet-A, and abdominal discomfort. Turbulence buffets her sturdy frame and the weary humans inside grimace. The wingtips shutter and rivets strain.

The motors' frenetic throbbing changes pitch and slows. The pilot is going through his checklist, configuring his old red and white airplane for smokejumper operations. Slowing down and descending from cruising speed. Flaps to 30%, speed to 110 knots, or something like that. I'm not a pilot.

The pressure in the young jumpers' ears change and the mood becomes tense. Conversations trail off. Pulses quicken. Pupils focus. Everyone knows what comes next...

The airplane slows and the whirring motors relax from a gallop to a canter. The air is denser and more palpable at 3,000 feet. The plane dips its wing towards a brooding new wildfire. The flames are nestled high against the slopes of the mountains. Smoke leans over steep and jagged ridgelines. It defuses and falls over the backside into a dizzying abyss. There are no easy answers to this one. The fire is in steep and treacherous terrain, and the jump-spot is very, very, small.

For the young jumpers inside the aircraft, the view breeds admiration and fear. The scenery is spectacular. Nature in all of its grandeur and remoteness, seen through an old scratched porthole in an old scratched airplane. Is the plane rotating around the mountains, or are the mountains spinning around the airplane? Hard to say.

The fear is primordial. It starts with a knot in the stomach and a weakness in the knees. Smiles fade. The amygdala is engaged and stress hormones are released. Dreadful, but also routine.

Silence, focus, inflection point.

A few salty words from a seasoned spotter, then game time.

Our young jumper purges himself from the plane. His lizard brain yearns for safety, warmth, comfort, and control, but his heart yearns for chaos, adventure, and validation. Heart wins. And besides, there is no going back. Wind rushes in his ears and the horizon wobbles and spins in his view.

He is not prepared. This is not to say that he has not been trained. He has. His equipment is fitted and well maintained. Procedural lists and algorithms rattle through his brain. He executes as he was taught. And yet, he is not prepared.

Emotions take over. The wrong ones.

The ground is rushing up. Motor functions become erratic and exaggerated. Thoughts, if present at all, are clipped, abrupt and contrite. The brain struggles to gain control, but in the end, it is merely reacting.

Input... Lag time... Output.

He's behind the ball and he knows it. His field of view narrows as though he is looking through a straw. Very little penetrates through his emotional defenses. Time warps, sounds become muffled, and the world spins.

Trees that were once too distant to draw his attention are now too big to look away from. Every branch and twig a threatening bayonet on which to impale himself, or worse, collapse his parachute and send him plunging to the mossy rocks below.

Evasive maneuver. Left, then right. Left again.

Absolution is mere seconds away.

I've been jumping for 13 years now. That doesn't make me salty, but I'm certainly no spring chicken either. I started in my 20s. At that age, you are filled with adrenaline and angst more than anything else. Certainly not wisdom, very little common sense, and definitely no humility. Bad decisions come easy when you are young, and luckily you can recover from most of them.

And so, it was for me. In the beginning, you don't really know what you are doing. You think you do, but you don't. Rookie training fills you with a lot of emotions. mostly fear, but also desire. Fear of what may happen when you thrust yourself from an airplane over the dense brooding forest. Desire to succeed, fit in, and thrive amongst your peers.

When you're new to anything you are vulnerable. The same goes for smokejumping. You are trying to build a skill, but you don't have the repetitions. You've got the drive, but you don't have the experience. And so, just like young men and women throughout time immemorial, what do you do? You just say, "Fuck it!", squint your eyes, clench all of your muscles, and launch into the unknown. Youth and inexperience beget arrogance and overconfidence.

Young jumpers almost always fall into this rutted path. Gripped by fear, they're inexperienced and tunnel-visioned. You may see them pumping their fists in the air and bashing their helmets together full of bravado. Or you may see them sitting silent and disengaged. Pupils small and lips pursed-in the pain cave.

It's only after 13 years that I can look back and see what I had been getting away with in those early days. The risks I was taking and the compensatory ways in which I dealt with them. Testosterone, bravado, and luck may carry the day, but humility will carry you through a season. Through a career. Through life.

Dirt Nap

Story by: Downtown Sarah Brown

It was 2002, and I was on the Biscuit Fire in southern Oregon. It was my first large fire, and I was happy as a clam. I was part of a 20-person handcrew working the night shift. The crazy thing is, the fire activity was so much more intense at night that we really couldn't do anything safely. So, we slept instead.

There was an incredible thermal belt where we were located that made it possible to lay on the bare ground in your yellow and be warm enough to catch some Z's, and we did just that. For about half of our roll, we ended up sleeping on the bare ground for at least a few hours a night, fully exposed to the warm summer air.

When I say I slept with my head in the dirt, what I mean is… I slept with my head in-the-dirt. Dirt is soft. It makes for a good pillow. Something I noticed during those nights with my head-in-the-dirt is that I had amazing dreams; the best dreams I've ever had. My 20-year-old, somewhat scientific brain, picked this apart and I developed a hypothesis. I believed that it was in fact, the smell of the dirt that brought on the good dreams. I mean, I love the smell of good soil. Who doesn't?

When I got home from that fire, I put my theory to the test and bought a bag of potting soil, put a pillowcase over it, and tossed it in my bed. While I couldn't actually sleep on the bag due to the crinkly noise it made, I was able to get plenty of dirt smell just having it right next to me as I slept. And guess what? I had good dreams! While my scientific methods were less than perfect, I did in fact, reach a conclusion: Sleeping with a dirt bag makes you have good dreams.

Nightly Comfort

Poem by: Andrew Foster Armstrong

I find that after a long day of work
With scorching heat all around
But especially above

The star-stricken night
Provides much needed rest
After a hard-fought fight

"Initial Attack" Pyrography on Ponderosa Pine
By Sheena Waters

The Chetco Effect

Story by: A. Taylor Johnson

My eyes are heavy during the five-hour drive. The hum of the fire engine increased as the straight-aways became more frequent on this coastal highway. The excitement between Slade and me is only a fraction of what it once was when we started our trip. That excitement faded into anxiety as we learned more about the fire summoning us. Just six hours prior, our supervisor called us over the radio asking if we'd be willing to take an off-district assignment. Our eyes lit up when he said, "You've been called to Chetco Bar."

The Chetco Bar fire started deep within Oregon's Kalmi-opsis National Forest, on July 12th, 2017. A lightning strike ignited the blaze in the old burn scars of the 1987 Silver fire and the 2002 Biscuit burn. Thousands of acres teeming with Sugar pines, Knobcone pines, Douglas firs, and Redwood trees -now dead and sun bleached shells of their former selves- were primed and ready to burn at nature's will. Helicopter rappellers had been dispatched to the fire and gave a good effort, but could not handle the waist-high manzanita brush that combusted with the flicker of a flame.

I followed the signs to fire camp just off Highway 101 through the town of Brookings. It stood proudly on the beach but, just a few miles away, a massive inferno knocked at its door. Thick Douglas fir trees lined the east side of town and waves crashed along the beaches to the west. I rolled down the windows to drown out the sound of Slade's snoring. His throaty rumble is something I ended up coping with during our 15 days at Chetco. Like the white noise of a fan or the crashing of waves, that snore would rock me to sleep whether I liked it or not.

Six in the morning came quickly after having just fallen asleep three hours before. The gravel-laden grass poked and prodded at my waist and ribs; a comfortable sleeping place was not a valid reason to keep me in bed on this morning. Slade told me to hurry up because the day shift briefing was about to begin. As I slid my Nomex fire pants onto each leg, my bare back brushed against the side of the tent and its ice-cold condensation shocked me awake. I rubbed the bags under my eyes and stepped into line with Slade.

Standing in the mob of men and women I managed to lose track of him, which was surprising because Slade towers at six and a half feet tall. I scanned the sea of worn-out faces and finally noticed his head poke out above the rest. With a paper coffee cup in each hand, he reached out to hand me one.

"Here, take this," he said.

I'm alright. I don't drink coffee.

"Are you sure?" He said with a look of surprise, "You're gonna be doing a lot of things here that you wouldn't normally do."

I'm sure. I really don't like it and I don't want to be 'that guy' who can't function without coffee.

"Alright brother, but you're gonna need it by tomorrow."

I tuned into the briefing as the chief meteorologist started presenting his fire weather forecast. He began to talk about the "Chetco Winds" which had prompted the influx of firefighters. We knew before that moment why we were there, but we didn't know exactly how this situation came to be.

The how, in this instance, was caused by something called "The Chetco Effect" or "The Chetco Winds." The Chetco winds are similar to the Santa Ana winds in California. This event, often called a Foehn wind, is the result of high-pressure building and pushing cold air downward. The push is so rapid that it heats the air and forces it to travel through favorable topography. The hot air dries out vegetation and fans the flames of relatively manageable wildfires into much larger ones. An event like this occurred in the early 20th century during the Great Fire of 1910. One account from the fire said, "The heat took my breath and claimed my home. Just over the hill, a column from hell engulfed the sky."

The Great Fire claimed over 3,000,000 acres in the Coeur d'Alene National Forest, most of it occurring in just 2 days. The Chetco winds fanned the Chetco Bar fire from 19,225 acres to 98,000 acres, just three days before we arrived.

Slade and I walked over to the break-out for Division Romeo so that we could meet our new division supervisor (DIVS); a stocky man of average height stood with a briefing packet in his hand. The bags under his eyes told me he'd been doing this awhile. The man greeted us with a lip full of chewing tobacco and a smile.

I do believe Slade could see what I also saw in him; a man who's seen it all. A man who doesn't carry an ounce of fear in his body. The DIVS Sup was a special kind of firefighter in our circle. A man shaped by fire and the type of man we aspired to be; a 'fire dog.'

Curious about his backstory I asked, "Hey, where are you from? And how long have you been doing this?"

"Well, I'm glad you asked," he said in a long drawl and grin from ear to ear, "I'm from Laramie, Wyoming. Been doing fire for about 23 years. Before this I did rodeo. So, you Oregon boys best not test me." I tried to act cool but laughed and fell back behind Slade's large frame. He let us know it was time to pack up our stuff and reconvene out on the fire in Division Romeo.

Division Romeo was located deep in the wilderness, away from the active flame front that threatened the town of Brookings. Thick clouds of dust coated our windshield as we drove along on dirt roads riddled with washboards. Excitement was building within me as I realized we were about to start a fight with the biggest wildfire in the United States. An elk leapt across the road out ahead of us so we stopped. There he stood, antlers high in the air and staring in our direction. His brown face and neck contrasted his sand-colored body; his legs blackened from ash and soot. My excitement faded to fear as we drove around a true champion of the forest.

The road turned rocky as we climbed the grade to Snow-camp lookout tower, soon surrounded by beautiful, centuries-old Redwood trees looming several hundred feet into the sky. Eventually, we crossed the threshold of sheltered forest to gaze upon the expanse of the Kalmiposis. Mosaic landscapes of Biscuit burn scars and living trees rolled through each peak. Three mushroom clouds played hide and seek behind the hills as we rolled through the narrow cut-out road. As the view opened up again, we finally got to see the whole picture. Combustible manzanita brush coated the mountainside leading up to the lookout. Steep drops seemed to pull the steering wheel toward them but I managed to keep a safe path. The fear in my body was nearly overwhelming, but my straight face refused to tell the truth. We parked at the base of the lookout to walk up the hill and meet with the DIVS Sup.

I grabbed my pack, cinching it around my waist and shoulders. The hill welcomed me to my first big fire, steep and choking me with smoke as I placed one foot in front of the other. Fear still sat inside of me, but I took solace in a quote from Gifford Pinchot, the first member of the U.S. Forest Service and arguably the first 'fire dog.' He said, "By acting as if I was not afraid, I gradually ceased to be afraid." Holding this in my mind, I crested the hill and, on top of being nearly breathless, I became speechless. Three black and grey columns reached for the heavens, each separated by their cardinal directions. To the east, a column was ripping across unstaffed wilderness. To the south, a mushroom cloud was chewing up the ground between us and it, while the column to the west threatened the city of Brookings. The ocean stretched toward the horizon in an expressionist painting of beauty and horror. Hell was knocking on our door and heaven wasn't so far away.

Hey, Slade?

"Yeah?"

I'm probably gonna need that coffee tomorrow.

"View from the Best Spike Camp" Pastel and Chalk,
By Anonymous

Recipe for Camaraderie

By: The Evolving Nomad

Supplies and Ingredients:

1- Enamel Coffee Pot
1- Bag of Coffee
1- 2.5-gallon Cubee of Water
1- Campfire
1- Crew of Folks
1- Spike Camp

Instructions:

The first to rise will get the warming fire started for the good
of the crew. The remaining crewmembers will wake up
one by one and begin to gather around said warming fire.
Volunteers of humanity will fill the coffee pot with water
nearly to the top and insert the pot into the warming fire.

While the water is working its way to a boil, crewmembers
will sit together in silence as the sun rises to their east.
Conversations will slowly begin to unfold as crewmembers
fiddle with their boots, tear open MRE packages, and adjust
their beanie hats.

Once the water has come to a boil, it will be removed from the fire by the most experienced maker of cowboy coffee, who will then:

1. Add the coffee to the top of the pot.
2. Briefly return it to the flame, then remove it again.
3. Once removed, cold water will be poured around the inner rim edges of the cowboy coffee pot, which will sink the grounds to the bottom.

The maker of the cowboy coffee will then pour coffee for their fellow crewmembers who have made comfortable seats of the dusty ground. The coffee will be consumed while circled up around a warming fire on a ridgetop and no one will miss their jetboil or their smartphone.

End Report.

Moonlighting

Tradition Hides LLC
Laura Grace Simon | Artist & Instructor
Rural Idaho

My journey to tanning hides using traditional methods started with a desire to personally connect with, and have a responsible hand in, the everyday alchemy in the world around us. During my many seasons as a fire lookout and working for backcountry ranches/outfitters in the off-seasons from fire, I have been witness to the slow, profound transmutation of forms extending beyond human lifetimes.

As a fire lookout, one is paid to pay deep attention to bigger picture process. This work illuminates connection in all beings and directly translates to tanning a hide. Often, what we humans consider as an end, is a beginning as well. Fire's role on the landscape continues to remind us that the death of one form, begets another.

In 2015, I began to spend my time at the lookout, working

with discarded hides I had scavenged from my off-season gigs. There are no chemicals involved, no shortcuts, or mass production. I tan hides using brains of wild animals, friction, elbow grease, wood smoke, and devotion. The lubricant in an animal brain is a water-soluble fat called phospholipids. When this combination of ingredients is physically applied to lubricate a hide's fibers, magic buckskin happens.

It requires strength to soften a hide. Traditional tanning is a practice never mastered. Every animal hide is a unique challenge and reflects the spirit the tanner themselves brings to the process. This hard work produces a soft durable chamois unmatched in quality. Tanning hides this way becomes a living testament of our connection to the land, all its critters, and to each other.

I love creating hunt talismans, moccasins, gloves, hoodies, bracelets, bags, and many other custom items. Brain-tanned buckskin pairs well with your infinite imagination. What I love most of all, is teaching this art to others. This art is meant to be shared, hand to hand within community. Walking others through the hide tanning process and starting their journey of connection to the materials in their own lives, brings me the most joy.

Thank you, deers.

Pursue curiosity here:
Email: *laughkillslonesome@gmail.com*
Instagram: *@traditionhides*

Pastime Leather Co.

Owner: D.B. Robbins

Twisp, WA.

Pastime Leather Co. began in the offseason (winter) of 2015. Leatherwork began as a creative outlet, and I quickly found that concentrating on something other than my day job was extremely beneficial to my mental wellbeing. I started out hand cutting, then saddle-stitching each item. This method doesn't require a bunch of fancy or expensive equipment- just the will to learn and to be okay with the inherent mistakes that come with the process. Each of the steps involved require the utmost care and attention to detail. One lapse in concentration, and the project usually ends up suplexed into the scrap bin, or perhaps used for target practice. Fairly recently, I bit the bullet and acquired a leather sewing machine, which allows me to produce very high quality work while still keeping prices reasonable. I thoroughly enjoy the challenge and reward of running a small business, and while also maintaining my "day job" as *Prevention Guy.* You CAN have it both ways, and have the freedom of choice.

If you are reading this thinking to yourself, "I would like to do something like that but... (enter excuse here)." Just take the first step. It can be challenging, but people in our line of work are not particularly known for backing down from a challenge.

You can find me at:
Website: *www.pastimeleatherco.com*
Instagram: *pastime_leather_co*
Email: *pastimehandbuilt@gmail.com*

FIRE LINGO GLOSSARY

AGL (Above Ground Level): AGL is an aviation reference. Example: Smokejumpers who use round parachutes exit the aircraft at 1,500 ft AGL, versus square chute jumpers who exit at 3,000 ft AGL.

Aerial Ignition: An ignition method where essentially flaming ping pong balls are dropped from a helicopter in specific patterns to help firefighters on the ground burn out large geographic areas.

AFMO (Assistant Fire Management Officer): An FMO manages the fire resources on a fire district. An AFMO is the position below the FMO. Example: A fire district has three engines and one handcrew, the FMO (or possibly AFMO) is their supervisor.

After Action Review (AAR): A formal or informal debriefing process of an event. The focus is to improve performance, while openly discussing the positives and negatives that may have taken place during said event.

Agency Administrator (AA): A person within the chain of command who has ultimate responsibility for an incident or geographic area. The fire chain of command will fall under an AA.

Air Attack (ATGS): Typically a fixed-wing aircraft is used to fly the air attack qualified personnel over an incident. The ATGS acts as an eye-in-the-sky to assist personnel on the ground with a different perspective of the incident, while also coordinating the incoming and outgoing aircraft above the fire.

Air Tanker: A plane (fixed-wing aircraft) that drops fire retardant.

Annual Leave: Annual leave is part of the vacation pay system for federal employees. An employee will accrue a few hours off per pay period, which builds up over time.

Aspect: The cardinal direction that a slope is facing. For example: If you are standing on a slope looking outward across the landscape, and the direction that you are looking is south, it means you are on the southern aspect.

Auger In: A commonly used phrase with aerially delivered firefighters, especially helicopter rappellers. It refers to generating too much speed on your descent and hitting the ground hard enough to hurt yourself.

Backburn: A fire that is set to burn away from your location with the wind.

Back Cut: When using a conventional cut to take down a tree with a chainsaw the sawyer would first cut a wedge out of the tree, called the "face cut." After the face cut has been made, the sawyer would then move the saw to the backside of the tree and make a back cut, which is what will make the tree fall.

Backing Fire: A fire that is burning against the wind and/or downslope is usually referred to as a *backing fire.*

Belt Weather Kit: A tool used by firefighters to take weather observations on an hourly basis throughout the day. Taking weather observations may also be referred to as slinging weather.

Bladder Bag: A backpack that is specifically designed to carry water. The backpack comes with a pump-action wand, which attaches to the backpack and allows the user to spray water onto hotspots. A full bladder bag generally weighs around 45 lbs. *Also referred to as a piss pump.*

Bone Pile: When firefighters take pieces of burning logs from within a section of the fire and pile them together (in a safe spot) so that they burn hot and cause complete consumption, that is referred to as a *bone pile*.

Box Canyon: A steep-sided, dead-end canyon.

Bucket: A collapsible bucket that attaches to the belly of a helicopter with a longline. The helicopter pilot dips the bucket into a water source and drops the water on flared-up areas of the fire. This is referred to as a "bucket drop."

Bucking: When a sawyer cuts a downed tree into smaller, more manageable chunks, or "rounds."

Buddy Check: A system check used with aerially delivered firefighters to ensure that all components of their life-bearing equipment have been properly configured. Two people come together and perform the check on one another.

Buggy: The boxy hotshot vehicles which can carry 10 people and a significant amount of fire gear are referred to as buggies.

Build Up: Or "Cell Build Up" is a reference to cumulus clouds building in the sky, which could be a sign of thunderstorms later in the day. Thunderstorm cells generate significant downdrafts and can create severe conditions on a wildfire. Storm cells are considered a serious watch-out for firefighters.

Bump:
1. Take a bump- This refers to moving up the distance of one person while building a fireline. It means that line construction is easier than it needs to be at the back of the line and the people in the front can move ahead to give them more work.
2. Bumping into the Green- Going to the bathroom outside of the fire perimeter. It is a cardinal sin to go to the bathroom in "the black" because firefighters put their bare hands in the ashen ground to search for areas that are holding heat.

Burnout: Setting a fire in order to consume fuel between the edge of the wildfire and the fireline. A burnout provides firefighters a bit more control of the fire behavior happening near the fireline, rather than allowing the wildfire to approach the fireline, and possibly move past it.

Burnover: A circumstance where firefighters become trapped by intense fire behavior with no way out. This is when a firefighter would deploy their fire shelter as a last resort for survival. The fire would then *burn over* them while they were inside their fire shelter.

Burn Scar: When a fire has burned through an area, the remnants are referred to by firefighters as a burn scar. For example, you might plan to let a fire burn up to the edge of the Tumwater fire burn scar because the fire will die out with no fuel to consume.

Cache: A storage area for firefighter supplies and equipment.

Canopy: The top portion of a tree where the leaves and/or needles reside.

Catface: When fire burns a concave into a tree's trunk, making the tree unstable that is called a catface.

Cargo Box: A box of firefighting supplies that either gets lowered from a helicopter (for rappellers), or released from an airplane (for smokejumpers). Cargo boxes include all the necessary firefighting equipment such as tools, chainsaw, fuel, medical kit, food, water, and miscellaneous supplies. A cargo box may also be referred to as a fire box and/or saw box, each holding their specified respective gear.

Cargo Chute: The type/size parachute that is specifically used for cargo boxes.

Cargo Drop: The aerial mission of releasing cargo out of an aircraft to deliver it to firefighters on the ground.

Cargo Letdown: The act of a spotter letting a cargo box down from a helicopter to the ground.

Ceiling: Ceiling is a term used in aviation that references the cloud level. Example: The ceiling is too low for the helicopter to fly.

Chain: A measure of distance, which is 66 ft. A chain is commonly referenced when building a fireline, and firefighters generally know how many of their own paces would equal one chain.

Chain of Command: The hierarchy of management levels within the firefighting organization. The chain of command is closely adhered to in firefighting. Hotshot Crew Example (Top to bottom): Superintendent, foreman, squad leader, senior firefighter, firefighter. If there is an issue you go upward in the chain of command one rung at a time until the issue has been resolved.

Chaparral: Chaparral is a thick, dense, shrub.

Chase Truck: The term is used interchangeably with a vehicle that carries crew supplies and equipment, or the vehicle that the overhead rides in. For helitack and rappel crews the chase truck is the vehicle that follows the helicopter to its final destination. It carries additional crewmembers and equipment to set up a helibase.

Check Line: A temporary fireline that is constructed in order to contain the fire while other tactics are being implemented, or additional resources are en route.

Chick Stick: *See Stick definition.* A chick stick is when both firefighters in the stick are women. Due to the low number of women in wildland firefighting, a chick stick tends to be rare.

Cliffed-Out: Working on wildfires in diverse terrain can sometimes find firefighters in a position where they come up against a cliff's edge, thereby hampering their efforts to move forward/down/up depending on the circumstance.

Climbers Left/Right: Generally used to describe a location when talking on the radio. Example: "The snag that needs to be cut down is upslope from your location by about 100 ft., climber's right."

Cold Front: A cold air mass moving in, displacing the warmer air. A forecasted cold front is a watch-out situation for firefighters because the wind intensifies and shifts directions, creating unpredictable and potentially extreme fire behavior.

Cold Trail: There are some fuel types that simply burn out with no real chance of spreading. In circumstances like these, firefighters will de-glove and run the backside of their hand along the burned edge of the fire, to feel for heat. It is a way to move quickly along the fire's edge so that focus can be placed on the areas that need real attention.

Column: The smoke plume that is visible above a fire is a column.

Comms: *Communications.* Aerial firefighters plug in and out of a *comms box* in the aircraft by the cord attached to their flight helmets. It's generally much too loud to communicate inside aircraft without using the avionics system.

Conduction: The transfer of heat through direct contact.

Contingency Line: A secondary fireline that is created as a backup when there is concern over the ability to hold the original fireline. Contingency line is essentially Plan B.

Contract Crews: While the majority of fire crews are either state or federal employees, there is also a sizeable portion of private industry fire resources who are hired contractually.

Convection: The transfer of heat by movement of a gas or liquid.

Creeping: Low fire intensity. When small flames "creep" along the forest floor burning surface fuels.

Crowning: *or Crown Fire.* When a fire is moving along in the tops of the trees completely independent of fire on the forest floor.

Cubee: A plastic bladder of drinking water encased in a cardboard box, which comes with a plastic handle for carrying. Firefighters typically slide the cubee onto their tool handle using the plastic handle to hike it to their work location. The standard volume of a cubee is 5 gallons, but smokejumpers and rappellers may pack 2.5 gallon cubees.

Cumulus Build-Up: Normally, cumulus clouds are not a concern for firefighters. However, when build-up turns into a cumulonimbus (tall anvil-shaped cloud), firefighters pay close attention, due to the potential for sudden downdrafts and gusty winds, which can dramatically affect fire behavior.

Cup Trench: When a fire is on a steep slope and there is danger of burning material rolling further down the slope and igniting a fire below, there is a need for a cup trench. A cup trench is built underneath the fire's edge on the downhill side. It is a deep v-shaped trench that is wide enough to catch rolling debris from the fire.

Cutting Line: Building/constructing fireline.

Daisy Chain: A way to transport something using multiple connected links.

DBH (Depth Breast Height): DBH is a term used when falling a tree. It refers to the circumference of a tree at breast height.

Dead and Down: Areas that have a significant amount of dead trees lying on the forest floor. The downed trees are usually crisscrossed and stacked on top of one another. This is commonly referred to as Jackstraw, Jim-Jam, or *Dead and Down.*

Dead Man's Curve: An aviation term that refers to the increased danger level of certain missions based on a calculation that accounts for height from the ground (AGL), and airspeed. Many common wildland fire missions happen within the *Dead Man's Curve.*

Demob: When a firefighter or fire resource (e.g. engine crew, hotshot crew) is leaving an incident due to lack of necessity or fulfilling their 14-day assignment they go through the "demob" process. *Demobilization; Officially checking out of the fire to begin travel home.

Descent Device: Helicopter rappellers use a rope and "descent device" to lower themselves from the helicopter to the ground.

Diggers: Crewmembers with hand tools who physically dig in the ground to construct a fireline. In a "line dig," firefighters are generally broken into two groups, the saws, and the diggers.

Direct Attack: Working to put the fire out along the fire's edge.

Dispatch: Fire dispatchers assign fire resources to respond to new fires, while also documenting fire size-ups relayed from the field, tracking firefighters' whereabouts, coordinating aircraft to respond to multiple fire incidents, and much more.

Division (DIVS):
1. A division is a geographical piece of ground. Large wildfires get broken up into divisions, which helps make a fire easier to manage. Fire resources then report to their respective *division.*
2. Division is also a qualified fire position. Each division of a fire has a division supervisor who manages the fire resources on that portion of the fire. Referred to as *Division,* or DIVS Sup.

Dolmar: A fuel container that has a compartment for chainsaw fuel, as well as bar oil.

Dozer Line: A fireline that has been created by a bulldozer.

Dozer Operator: Bulldozers are used regularly in firefighting operations. Dozer operators need to be very skilled in order to navigate the difficult terrain, as well as the additional hazards associated with wildfire.

Drip Torch: A firing device used regularly by firefighters in burnout operations. A drip torch is a handheld metal can (approximately 15-20 lbs when full) with a long wick to drip fuel. Firefighters ignite the wick and literally drip fire onto the ground as they hike along.

Dry Run: Before a retardant plane makes a drop, a dry run is performed to show the intended path and placement.

Dual Career: If both partners in a relationship have a fire career it's referred to as *dual career.*

Duff: The layer of decomposing leaf litter that sits just above the mineral soil layer. Fire can smolder in duff for a long time, given the opportunity.

Duty Officer (DO): A person who is the on-call point of contact for dispatch if there is a reported smoke (fire). The DO will then either go scout the smoke themselves or have dispatch send fire resources to assess the situation.

Eddy: Circling air or water that resides on the backside of a solid obstacle such as a mountain ridgeline, or large boulder in a river is called an *eddy.*

ELT: *Emergency Locator Transmitter.* An ELT is affixed to aircraft in case of a hard landing or crash.

Engine Crews: An engine crew generally consists of 3-7 people who usually work along road systems. Engine crews are invaluable in the "urban interface" setting when structures (homes, buildings, etc.) are being threatened by an advancing wildfire.

Entrapment: When firefighters have been enclosed by a fire with no way out. An entrapment may, or may not necessitate the use of fire shelters.

ERC Chart: *Energy Release Component* Chart. ERC Charts are used by firefighters to reference historical fire activity relative to weather and dryness of fuel, based on the date.

Escape Route: A pre-established route that has been flagged and made clear of obstacles so that firefighters can quickly leave the area they are working and make way to the safety zone if necessary.

Face Cut: When using a conventional cut to fall a tree with a chainsaw the sawyer would first cut a wedge out of the tree, called the "face cut." After the face cut has been made, the sawyer would then move the saw to the backside of the tree and make a back cut, which is what will make the tree fall.

Faller: A person who has been trained and certified to cut down trees. There are different levels of certification, from novice to highly experienced. Firefighters may be qualified to cut down hazardous trees as well.

Fine Fuels: Fine fuels are essentially the kindling to a forest fire. They are the easiest to catch fire and will generate enough heat to help catch heavier fuels on fire. Fine fuels are also referred to as light flashy fuels. Strong winds mixed with light flashy fuels can be quite dangerous and/or destructive.

Fingers: Depending on the way a fire burns it may burn in such a way as to create "fingers." Typically, firefighters will burnout a section of unburned fuel to make the fire's circumference more circular. Dealing with long fingers on a fire expends much more time and effort for firefighters.

Firebrand: A firebrand is a burning ember that has the potential to ignite unburned fuel if it is blown across the fireline into "the green."

Firebreak: An area that is cleared of combustible fuel. A firebreak (or fuel break) can be human-created or natural.

Fireline: A fireline is similar in appearance to a hiking trail. A fireline encircles a fire and removes the ability of the fire to continue spreading by digging/scraping away fuel down to the mineral soil layer. The width of a fireline will vary greatly depending on the fuel type, topography, and fire behavior.

Fire Assignment: When a firefighter leaves on an out-of-area fire assignment, more than likely that person will be gone for at least 14 days. Firefighters could get extended to 21 days if there's a need. Another possibility is that after working for 14 days, the fire crew could take "R+R" days in area local to the fire before working an additional 14 days, and then returning home.

Fire Camp: Fire camp is essentially a tent city. Fire camp and ICP (incident command post) can sometimes be used interchangeably, but they are not always in the same location as one another. Fire camp provides resources for firefighters such as food, supplies, and designated sleeping areas, while ICP is wherever the IMT (incident management team) has set up their command post.

Fire Gear: Also referred to as line gear, line pack, or fire pack. Essentially, fire gear is the fire backpack that is worn on the fireline. However, fire gear may also encompass PPE like boots, helmet, and a tool.

Fire Triangle: The fire triangle consists of the three components necessary to make a fire-fuel, heat, and oxygen.

Fire Scar: When a fire has burned through an area, the remnants are referred to by firefighters as a fire scar, and/or burn scar. Example: you might plan to let a fire burn up to the edge of the Tumwater fire scar because the fire will die out with no fuel to consume.

Fire Season: The time of year when weather aligns with dry forest vegetation is fire season. Fire season takes place at different times of the year depending on the geographic region of the country/world. With each passing year fire season is expanding due to warmer climates and dry vegetation turning fire season into more of a "fire year."

Fire Shelter: A lifesaving piece of PPE carried by American wildland firefighters as a last resort tool. If a firefighter was on the verge of being burned over by a fire, they could deploy this multi-layered heat shield, and crawl inside in an attempt to survive the flaming front and super-heated gases.

Fire Qualifications: A person's fire qualifications are listed on their "red card." Qualifications are gained after a firefighter has taken the appropriate classes and successfully completed the "taskbook" associated with the qualification. Fire qualifications are also referred to as quals.

Fire Whirl: Essentially a fire tornado that has the potential to carry debris, smoke, and flame over the fireline and into unburned fuel. Fire whirls can vary greatly in size.

Firing Operation: When firefighters intentionally light a fire for a specific purpose.

Flank: A wildfire has a head, two flanks, and the heel. The flanks are either side of the fire.

Flare Up: A flare-up usually occurs when the surface fire has been pre-heating ladder fuels and they finally dry and begin to catch fire.

Flight Following: The process through which an aircraft is tracked from departure point to destination. Flight following provides the aircraft's location at regular time intervals in case of an event or mishap. This way, the aircraft can be located quickly during the search and rescue. Additionally, Automated Flight Following (AFF) is a system in which the aircraft is followed via computer tracker so that the dispatcher (or person following the flight) can see the aircraft's location on a map.

Flight Suit: A coverall type outfit that is worn over clothing during flights.

FMO (Fire Management Officer): An FMO manages the fire resources on a fire district. Example: A fire district has three engines and one handcrew, the FMO is their supervisor.

Foehn Wind: A warm, dry, and strong seasonal wind that takes place in certain geographical areas. A wind of this type can create critical fire weather conditions. Foehn winds are called by different names according to the geographic location; such as Santa Ana winds in Southern California.

Fold-a-Tank: A Fold-A-Tank is a collapsible water storage system that can be transported by truck or helicopter to remote locations, in order to provide firefighters with a water source.

Food Box/Bag: A food box/bag is a food supply provided to smokejumpers and rappellers that should last each firefighter 72 hours.

Foreman: Second in command on a fire crew.

Fresh Food Box: A large box of fresh food ingredients is provided regularly via cargo drop to firefighters in the backcountry of Alaska.

Fuel:
1. Combustible material, which includes vegetation such as grass, leaves, ground litter, plants, shrubs, and trees. All of which fuel a wildfire.
2. Fuel: Actual fuel used for chainsaws, water pumps, etc.

Fuel Cycle: Fuel cycle is an aviation term. In wildfire, it's used to reference the duration of time a pilot can work for you. Example: When a helicopter arrives on scene, the firefighter might ask over the radio, "where are you in your fuel cycle?" and the pilot will respond with an approximation of how much longer they can fly before having to set down the aircraft to refuel.

Fuel Moisture Content: A calculated percentage of water content found in vegetation. The fuel moisture content lets firefighters know how available fuel is to burn. The less fuel moisture, the higher the fire danger.

Fusee: A strikeable flare that is commonly carried in fireline packs and used in small-scale firing operations.

Fuselage: The main body of an aircraft.

GACC: Geographic Area Coordination Center.

Green: Being green refers to a new firefighter. A rookie firefighter. *See:* "The Green" for additional definition.

Greens: Firefighters often refer to their Nomex fire pants as their *greens.* Nomex pants are a PPE requirement for the fireline.

Gridding: *Or Grid* is a formal search formation. In fire, a grid formation is generally used to walk through an unburned area looking for spot fires or to search through a burned area for remaining heat/smoke.

Haines Index: An index that is referenced by firefighters to help them predict potential fire growth. The Haines Index functions on a scale that measures between 2-6; 6 being the highest potential for large fire growth.

H-pay: Hazard pay is referred to as H-pay. H-pay is an additional pay bump that is granted when engaged on a wildfire.

Handcrew: A group of approximately 10-20 firefighters who work together consistently throughout the fire season. Typically, firefighters continue to work on the same crew for several years in a row.

Handline: A fireline built with hand tools.

Head of the Fire: The side of the fire with the fastest rate of spread.

Heavy Fuels: Larger circumference dead trees and logs are considered heavy fuels. Even if heavy fuels are dried out, they still require pre-heating before being able to catch fire.

Heel of the Fire: The back of the fire, opposite from the "head" of the fire.

Helibase: Helibase is essentially the incident command post for aviation resources. It is also the physical ground where rotor-wing aircraft (helicopters) that are assigned to a specific incident take off, land, and park overnight.

Helispot: A space in the forest that has been cleared to certain specifications so that a helicopter may land in the backcountry safely.

Helitack: Firefighters who utilize a helicopter as their mode of transportation to deliver them to a wildfire.

Hold and Improve:
1. A command used during fireline construction, which signifies the need to stop forward progress.
2. Slang for "sit around and wait for an undetermined amount of time." Find something to keep you busy for awhile.

Holder: A firefighter who is standing on the fireline looking for spot fires while a burnout operation is going on.

Holdover Fire: Lightning storms that produce ground strikes can start fires. It's not unusual for a fire to smolder, not showing smoke for several days, before finally being spotted by a fire lookout. This type of new start would be called a *holdover fire.*

Hose Lay: An extensive connection of several lengths of fire hose is called a hose lay. The hose gets carried into the forest by firefighters, then assembled on the ground beginning at the water source. The water source could be a fire engine, a fold-a-tank, a stream/river, etc.

Hotshot Crew: A 20+ person handcrew. Hotshot crews are required to maintain specific fitness levels and fire qualifications. Hotshot crews are a highly regarded, Type 1, firefighting resource.

Hung-Up Tree: When a tree has started to fall over but got stuck in the tops of other trees on its way down it is "hung up." This poses a hazard to firefighters since the base of the tree is not secure and the tree could break loose and come down at any time.

IA (Initial Attack): When a fire starts, the firefighters first on scene are considered to be the initial attack resource. In this circumstance, firefighters regularly say they are I.A.'ing a fire.

IA Crew: IA Fire crews are dispatched to be first on scene of a new fire.

IAP (Incident Action Plan): An IAP is used by firefighters on large incidents to reference communications plans, resources, maps, emergency medical information, etc.

IC (Incident Commander): The incident commander is the person in charge of a fire. The larger the fire is, an IC may have support staff under them, such as operations, plans, logistics, etc.

ICP (Incident Command Post): The ICP is the geographic location where an incident management team sets up its operations. The ICP is usually in the same place as "fire camp," which is essentially a base camp for firefighters.

ICS (Incident Command System): ICS is used to organize chaotic situations by establishing a chain of command, as well as parameters for workload, number of subordinates, etc.

IMT (Incident Management Team): An IMT is a group of specially qualified people to organize and maintain control of large fire incidents.

Indirect Attack: A method of fire suppression where a fireline is constructed far ahead of the fire's edge for the fire to eventually run into.

Inversion: An atmospheric condition that will cause smoke to settle into valleys, or low-lying areas until the inversion lifts. An inversion generally lifts by early-to-mid afternoon, but an inversion could remain for several days, creating issues for aviation resources.

IR: Infrared heat detection system.

IRPG (Incident Resource Pocket Guide): All firefighters carry an IRPG with them while fighting fire. It is a valuable quick guide commonly referenced for information such as proper helispot circumference, etc.

Island: An unburned area within a fire's perimeter (also known as a pocket) is referred to as an *island.*

Jackstraw: Areas that have a significant amount of dead trees lying on the forest floor. The downed trees are usually crisscrossed and stacked on top of one another. This is commonly referred to as *Jackstraw*, Jim-Jam, or Dead and Down.

Jet-A: Fuel used for aircraft.

Jim-Jam: Areas that have a significant amount of dead trees lying on the forest floor. The downed trees are usually crisscrossed and stacked on top of one another. This is commonly referred to as Jackstraw, *Jim-Jam*, or Dead and Down.

Jumper: Smokejumper.

Jump Gear: Smokejumper suit. Jump gear consists of a large, bulky, pale-yellow suit made from Kevlar and hockey padding. Jump gear also includes a helmet (with face cage), flight gloves, a reserve, and a main parachute.

Jump Spot: The area that has been designated by the spotter as the place for smokejumpers to land.

Ladder Fuels: Mid-height fuels that help a fire go from ground/surface fuels, up to the tops of the trees are called *ladder fuels.*

LAL (Lightning Activity Level): LAL is part of the National Fire Danger Rating System (NFDRS) and is in reference to the probable frequency of cloud-to-ground lightning strikes.

LCES (Lookout-Communication-Escape Routes-Safety Zones): It is considered bad business to engage in a wildfire without first establishing these four safety measures.

Lead Plane: Aircraft/pilot that makes trial runs over the target areas of a fire prior to the air tanker itself. Lead planes also guide air tankers through a drop.

Letdown Lines: Tubular webbing that is used to lower cargo from an aircraft. Letdown line is also used by smoke-jumpers when they land in a tree. They use it to build a makeshift harness and lower themselves to the ground.

Lighter: A firefighter who is one of the people carrying a drip torch and dropping dots of fire in the forest during a burnout operation.

Lightning Bust: Lightning storms have the potential to create multiple new fires. When this happens, firefighters refer to it as a *lightning bust.*

Line: Shorthand for fireline.

Line Dig: The construction of a fireline by a group of people. A line dig could consist of any number of people depending on the circumstance.

Line gear/pack: A firefighter's backpack of gear, which is carried with them on the fireline at all times.

Line Order: Handcrews (especially hotshot crews) have an order in which crewmembers line up to dig fireline and/or hike. The order is generally kept the same for the entire fire season with few exceptions. This means that the people in front and back of you while you're in line, will always be the same. The order is developed based on which tool each person has been assigned and where it will be complementary in a line dig as compared to other tools.

Load:
1. A load of smokejumpers and/or rappellers. The amount of people in a load depends on the type of aircraft being used.
2. Retardant load. An aircraft will drop a retardant load on a fire to help slow the fire's spread.
3. Sling load. Cargo that is carried beneath a helicopter and attached by a long line and swivel.

Longline: A cable/wire line (at least 50 ft in length) that can be attached to the underside (belly) of a helicopter, for use in picking up and dropping off cargo nets full of equipment in the field.

Long-Range Spotting: Firebrands can travel long distances away from the fire, creating new fire starts. Firebrands can easily travel 1/4 mile or more, from the main fire.

Lookout:
1. A person designated to detect and report fires from a lookout tower.
2. A location from which fires can be detected and reported.
3. A fire crewmember assigned to observe the fire from a vantage point and warn crewmembers when there is potential danger.

Manifest: A manifest is required for all flights to determine how much weight will be onboard. Passenger names are listed on the manifest as well as itemized cargo such as hazardous material. Qualified firefighters build flight manifests and present them to the pilot before take-off.

Manpurse: Most firefighters carry a "manpurse." It is a small Velcro organizer that can fit into a cargo pant pocket. A manpurse generally contains an IRPG, notepad, pen, sharpie, and Smokey calendar to keep track of hours worked.

Mark-3 Pump: A mark 3 pump is a portable pump that can be dropped to firefighters when a nearby water source is available.

MIST (Minimum Impact Suppression Tactics): A method of firefighting used to create minimal disturbance of the natural environment. MIST tactics are commonly used in designated wilderness areas.

Mock-Ups: Smokejumpers utilize mock-ups prior to an operational mission in an unfamiliar aircraft, while helicopter rappellers perform mock-ups in training. In either case, a mock-up allows the firefighter to have a "dry run" with the aircraft stationary on the ground in order to gain familiarity before going "live."

Moonscape: When a fire blankets thick gray ash on the forest floor for as far as the eye can see it is referred to as moonscape because it looks similar to being on the moon.

Mop-Up: After a fire has burned through an area, firefighters work the perimeter edges and/or the entire burned area (depending on the size of the fire) with hand tools -and sometimes water- to extinguish lingering pockets of heat. Mop-up is slow tedious work for firefighters.

MRE (Meal Ready to Eat): MREs are prepackaged meals, which were originally developed for the military to help meet the need of an extended shelf life and high-calorie content.

Natural Barrier: Any natural feature on the landscape that lacks flammable material and/or can obstruct the fire's spread. May also be referred to as a "firebreak."

Needle Cast: Pine needles that have been shed from trees.

New Start: New wildfire.

NICC: National Incident Coordination Center.

NIFC: National Interagency Fire Center.

Nomex: Nomex is the fire-resistant material that fire pants and fire shirts are made of. Nomex is required to be worn when on the fireline.

NWCG: National Wildfire Coordinating Group.

Off-Season: The winter months in the U.S. are generally considered the off-season. Seasonal firefighters are laid-off during the winter months, while firefighters who are employed year-round try to take a vacation before it disappears. This is a government agency phenomenon called "use or lose," where vacation time has a time limit and then goes away.

Old Schools: When a firefighter refers to "old schools," they are talking about a pair of Nomex pants and/or a Nomex shirt, from the 1960s or 70s.

Ops (Operations):
1. The unit within the Incident Command System- Operations
2. The person heading the operations unit is referred to as Operations or Ops.
3. Operations. The functional act of doing something out on the fireline.

Ops Normal: Ops normal is generally used as sarcastic commentary about how things might be a complete mess, but messy is normal, and everyone is used to dealing with it.

Overhead: Overhead refers to the supervisors above you. Example: A crewmember's overhead would be the superintendent and foreman and/or crewboss and assistant crewboss.

Pack Out: Refers to how smokejumpers and/or rappellers get their gear off of a remote wildfire. Firefighters pack all their fire gear/supplies into large packout bags, then hike across the landscape to reach a feasible pick-up point. A standard pack-out bag weighs approximately 85-110 lbs.

Pack Out Bag: A large bag that firefighters pack fire gear/ supplies in, so they can hike it out of the forest.

Pack Test: The required annual physical endurance test for all fireline personnel. There are variations of the pack test depending on designated functions. However, arduous duty firefighters are required to complete a 3-mile walk on flat ground within 45 minutes, while carrying 45 lbs on their person.

Parts of a Fire: There are generally five parts of a fire. The heel, the head, the right/left flanks, and the point of origin. The heel is the back, the head is the front, the right/left flanks are the sides, and the point of origin is where the fire started.

Perm: Permanently employed wildland firefighter.

PG Bag (Personal Gear Bag): The issued bag that is used by firefighters to store 14 days' worth of their personal belongings. Also sometimes referred to as a red bag.

P-Line: A shortcut access trail that firefighters may build to make travel to/from the fire's edge quicker and easier.

PLF (Parachute Landing Fall): A PLF is a skill set taught to smokejumpers to help prevent landing injuries.

Point of Origin: The spot where the fire started, which could have come from a lightning strike, a spark, arson, etc.

PPE (Personal Protective Equipment): Different tasks within firefighting require different components of PPE. For example, all firefighters are required to wear a helmet when out on the fireline, but only sawyers and swampers are required to wear saw chaps.

Prescribed Fire/Burn: A fire that is intentionally set in order to benefit the health of the forest and/or improve animal habitat. A written and approved prescribed fire plan must exist prior to ignition. Also called an RX burn.

Pre Po/Pre-position. When fire resources have been called to a geographic area with high fire danger due to the likelihood of new fire starts, it is referred to as a *pre-po* assignment.

Pre-treat: The use of water, foam, or retardant along a fire-line in advance of the fire.

PSE (Permanent-Seasonal Firefighter): A firefighter who gets retirement and benefits, but is laid off for one-to-four months each year.

Pulaski: A combination tool that can be used for digging, trenching, or chopping. Pulaskis are the most universally utilized tool on the fireline.

Quals: *Qualifications.* A person's fire qualifications are listed on their "red card." Quals are gained after a firefighter has taken the appropriate classes and successfully completed the "taskbook" associated with the qualification.

Rappeller: A Type 1 firefighter that is flown by helicopter to remote and difficult to reach fires, then inserted into the fire by rappelling down a rope from the helicopter.

Rappel Spot: The spot that has been designated by the spotter for the rappellers to land in.

Rate of Spread: The term rate of spread is relative to the growth of a fire's size. Firefighters usually reference how many chains per hour the fire is burning to give a frame of reference for the fire activity. *See* "chain" definition.

Ready Load: Refers to the group of firefighters who are first up on the rotation board for a fire. Smokejumpers and rappellers both operate from a rotation board and the ready load consists of the number of people that can fit with regard to the aircraft's capacity.

Re-burn: Small remote fires that are responded to by smokejumpers and/or rappellers are required to be put out 100% since remote fires cannot be patrolled later. If one of these remote fires is still holding any heat, there is potential for a *re-burn*, which means the same fire has started back up again. It's considered to be quite embarrassing to have a re-burn on one of your fires.

Ready Shack/Ready Room: The place where smokejumpers and/or rappellers stage their gear in a manner that makes it easier for them put on when the alarm sounds to respond to a fire.

Recon: To scout out ahead of fire resources. Firefighters regularly take recon flights to get an aerial view of a fire.

Red Card: A small pocket-sized card that wildland firefighters carry with them, which is essentially their license to fight fire. The red card lists which qualifications the firefighter is certified for, as well trainee status positions.

Red Flag Warning: A term used by fire weather forecasters to alert firefighters of a critical fire weather threat.

Refurb: *Refurb* usually refers to getting gear "fire ready" after it has been used.

RH (Relative Humidity): RH helps firefighters determine the prime burning hours of the day. Fires burn the easiest during points of the day when RH is at its lowest.

Repeater: A radio signal station that relays a transmission so the message can travel a further distance. Repeaters are open channels, which means the communication can be heard by an entire forest if they are scanning that repeater channel.

Resource Order: The official form that is used to order resources to a fire. The resource (crew, engine, etc.) brings the resource order with them to the incident and use it to check in to the incident.

Retardant Drop: Fire retardant that is dropped from a plane or heli-tanker over portions of a fire to help calm the flames is called a retardant drop.

Rhino: A specially designed firefighting hand tool.

Rock Scree: A large boulder field typically on the side of a slope, that has no combustible fuel to catch fire.

Roll: Slang for fire assignment. A firefighter might say that they are "headed out on a *roll,*" which means that they'll more than likely be gone for at least 14 days.

Rotation Board: Smokejumpers and rappellers list all their firefighters on a rotation board at the beginning of the season (usually by drawing numbers out of a hat) and everyone stays in that order for the duration of the fire season. It determines who is next up for a fire assignment. The *rotation board* is considered to hold your fate for the season, for better or worse.

Rotor Wash: The air turbulence that occurs under a hovering helicopter. Rotor wash can be so significant that it can break out tree branches, knock over small-diameter trees, kick up a significant amount of dust, and/or intensify fire activity.

Round: When a log is cut into smaller chunks, those chunks are referred to as *rounds.*

Running Saw: Using a chainsaw.

SA (Situational Awareness): A term that is commonly used in firefighting to promote constant observation of the situation as well as your surroundings in relation to potential hazards.

Saddle: A saddle-shaped depression along the ridgeline of a hill/mountain between two higher points.

Safety Zone: When fire activity becomes extreme firefighters may need to retreat to a safety zone. An area that has been pre-identified by firefighters as a place relatively free of combustible material, and large enough for firefighters to safely wait out the intensified fire behavior.

Saw Line: A wide swath in the forest, which is cut by a fire crew's sawyers, ahead of the crew's digging squad. Saw line removes brush/fuel to help slow the fire before it reaches the fireline.

Saw Team/Partner: A saw team could consist of two sawyers who take turns cutting with the chainsaw (usually cutting for a full fuel tank and then switching), while the other person acts as their swamper. Or the saw team could consist of one sawyer and one swamper.

Sawyer: A sawyer is a person who has been certified to operate a chainsaw. Sawyers have varying experience and training levels and are certified based on skill.

Seasonal: Seasonally employed firefighter.

Scope of Duty: Qualifications, experience level, and position title all play a factor in one's scope of duty. To be operating outside of your scope of duty signifies that you have not been adequately trained for that responsibility, and/or the circumstances surpass capacity. This can happen when a fire is growing rapidly and there is a need to transition to a more experienced IC. The acting IC can choose to continue in that capacity until the transition, or they can choose to disengage. Either is acceptable so long as the acting IC is still within their comfort zone.

Scratch Line: A very basic fireline that is used as an emergency measure to check the spread of fire. Most often used when the fire is moving quickly and there aren't enough firefighters to staff the fire.

Secret Squirrel Channel: A secret squirrel channel is a radio frequency where the transmissions can only be heard between the members of one particular crew.

Shot Crew: *Hotshot crew.*

Sigg: A small fuel bottle that looks similar to a metal water bottle.

Six-Hour Watch: The long-held tradition for small remote wilderness fires was to put the fire completely out and then sit and watch it for 6 hours. If a smoke popped up during the *six-hour watch*, the watch would start over again. This helped ensure that a fire would not restart after firefighters had left it.

Sizes of Fires: Fires are categorized as Type 5 through 1 in reference to size. A Type 5 fire is the smallest and least complex, while a Type 1 fire is the largest and most complex.

Size-Up: Firefighters will *size-up* a fire by scouting around the perimeter and taking several factors into account for the best course of action before resources engage on the fire.

Skier's Left/Right: Generally used to describe a location when talking on the radio. Example: "The snag that needs to be flagged is downslope from your location by about 100 ft., skier's right."

Slash: Slash refers to heavy amounts of down debris on the forest floor. It could have been generated from weather events, logging operations, etc.

Slicked Off Black: Slicked off black refers to an area where the fire has completely consumed all vegetation.

Sling Load: Cargo carried beneath a helicopter and attached by a line and swivel.

Sling Psychrometer: A hand-operated instrument for obtaining wet and dry bulb temperature readings and, subsequently, relative humidity. Using this method is commonly referred to by firefighters as slinging weather, or spinning weather.

Slopover: When part of a fire crosses over the fireline where it was meant to keep from advancing, that is considered a *slopover*.

Smokejumper: A Type 1 firefighter that is flown by plane to remote and difficult to reach fires, then inserted into the fire by parachuting from an airplane.

Snag: A standing dead tree, burned or unburned. Snags present a hazard on the fireline and identifying them and/

or removing them is important to firefighter safety.

Soup Sandwich: A term used to reference a person who is essentially a hot mess.

Spike Camp: A smaller, more primitive version of a fire camp that is set in a remote location. Spike camps are set up to lessen the commute time of firefighters to certain portions of the fire. Spike camps generally provide food, water, and some basic supplies. A spike camp can also consist of one single crew and very basic provisions, such as MREs, drinking water, and chainsaw fuel. When this is the case, it's referred to as spiking out.

Spiked Out: When a fire resource sleeps on/very near the fire's edge with very little logistical support.

Spooled Up: When a helicopter's rotors are turning while it is sitting on the ground, it's considered *spooled-up* and ready to go. This saying can also refer to someone's attitude. "They got all *spooled-up* about it!"

Spot Fire: A small fire that starts up outside the main fire due to a firebrand crossing over the fireline into receptive fuels.

Spotter: A person who is charged with designating a jump or rappel spot, interacting with the pilot, and sending jumpers or rappellers out of their respective aircraft through hand signals and/or verbal commands.

Spotter Check: A safety gear check performed by a spotter before a live operation.

Spotting:
1. When firebrands from the main fire are carried by the wind, land in unburned fuel, and ignite new smaller fires, that is referred to as *spotting*. Spot fires can vary greatly in size.
2. When jumpers or rappellers load up and fly off to respond to an initial attack fire, the spotter would be considered to be "spotting a load."

Spur Ridge: Topographically, there are "main ridges" that are essentially the spine or backbone of a mountain. A spur ridge is a small off-chute of the main ridgeline. There are generally several spur ridges on any one mountain.

Squad: Usually made up of 5-7 people. A crew of 20 people breaks down into smaller squads, each with their own respective squad leader.

Squaddie: *Squad leader.*

Squad Boss: *Squad leader.* The supervisor of 5-7 people when the larger crew gets split up for work assignments.

Stable vs. Unstable Atmosphere: In relation to firefighting, fires burn hotter and with more intensity when the atmosphere is unstable and you can expect poor visibility due to smoke when the atmosphere is stable.

Staff Ride: A valuable learning tool where firefighters visit the location of a fatality fire to get a clearer understanding of what happened. Typically, some firefighters who were directly involved in the incident attend in order to provide students of fire with first-hand knowledge.

Staging: *See:* Pre-Po and Staging Area.

Staging Area: A geographical location where fire resources are placed to wait for their assignment.

Stick: "A Stick" refers to two people exiting an aircraft together. Smokejumpers exit the aircraft in *sticks*, as do helicopter rappellers.

Superintendent: The highest-ranking person on a hotshot crew.

Sup: Short for the title of Supervisor. Example: I just talked to the Forest Sup and she said...

Swamper: A swamper is a person who works with a sawyer to help them clear away brush and debris as they cut and buck trees.

Switchback: Sometimes hiking trails are built where they essentially zig zag back and forth up a slope. Switchbacks are used to help lessen the effort to reach the top when a slope is steep.

Swivel: A metal hook that swivels in either direction. It's used to configure the long line for transporting sling loads of cargo by helicopter.

Taskbook: In order for any firefighter to become certified for fire qualifications they must first complete the tasks within the taskbook for that specific qualification. Generally, each task (of which there are several in any one taskbook) needs to be performed competently three times before being "signed off."

Team: Short for incident management team (IMT). An IMT comes to take control of a fire when it has grown past the capacity of local resources to manage.

TFR (Temporary Flight Restriction): A TFR is a restricted airspace placed over a wildfire, and put into effect by the Federal Aviation Administration (FAA). The restriction is requested by fire officials so that nonessential aircraft don't fly into the airspace above a fire. TFRs protect fire pilots from potentially crashing with civilian aircraft.

The Black: "The black" is the area that a wildfire has already burned through. It could be referred to as clean black if the fire consumed everything cleanly, or skunky/dirty black if the fire left vegetation that could catch fire again later.

The Green: "The green" refers to areas that have not been burned. The green is what firefighters are trying to protect. If firefighters were performing a grid search for spot fires they would be walking through *the green*.

Thermal Belt: A geographic area, usually toward the upper third of a mountain, where the temperatures stay relatively warm throughout the night, rather than cooling down.

Tied-In: The act of connecting one section of fireline to another section of fireline or natural barrier. Oftentimes multiple fire resources are working simultaneously on different portions of the fire and work until they meet one another, essentially, tying in the line. Firefighters also tie in with one another to have a conversation or to come up with a plan.

Torching: When a single tree or a small group of trees catch fire in a flaring fashion, after being cured to burn by the surrounding ground fire.

TU (Tits Up): When somebody "goes down" on the fireline from overexertion or heat stress, firefighters say the person went TU.

Travel Pants: Most fire crews are required to travel home from a fire assignment in "clean greens." They are referred to as travel pants because firefighters will only wear them on their travel home. Because of this, firefighters might use old school Nomex pants as their travel pants, because they are too delicate to wear on the fireline but very comfortable.

Two More Chains: A chain is a measure of distance. A firefighter might ask how much further they have to go until they tie in the fireline they are building. The answer they get will probably be, "two more chains," meaning we aren't there yet, but we're getting close. Of course, it's never only two more chains.

Type: Refers to resource capability. A Type 1 resource might provide more power, size, capacity, qualifications, etc.; than would be found with a Type 2 resource. Resource typing helps standardize fire equipment and resources, which makes it easier for people to understand what they are ordering.

UAS (Unmanned Aircraft System): *Also known as drones.* Wildland firefighters use drones in multiple ways in assistance of fire operations.

UB (Union Break): Someone might say they are taking a UB when they sit down and grab a snack.

Underburn: A fire that consumes surface fuels but not the overstory canopy in a forest.

Underslung Line: A fireline that is placed below a fire that is burning on a slope. Underslung line can present several problems due to the potential that burning material might roll out, below the fire, starting a new fire further down the hill.

Use-or-Lose: A term referring to time off. Many firefighters don't have the luxury of taking time off during the year so their vacation hours accumulate. The government will take those hours away if they aren't used by a certain date, so firefighters tend to "burn" their use-or- lose in November and December before it disappears.

Virga: Precipitation falling out of a cloud, that evaporates before it reaches the ground.

Water Tender: A ground vehicle which transports large volumes of water to strategic locations. Water tenders may also be used to dampen down very dusty areas prior to helicopters landing/taking-off, etc.

Wet Line: A line of water, or water/chemical retardant, that gets sprayed along the ground to act as a temporary control line. It can help to slow a fire down temporarily.

Widowmaker: A portion of a tree/limb that is stuck in the branches of another tree. The fact that it could fall out at any time, potentially killing a person, is why it is called a widowmaker.

Wildfire Module (WFM): Wildfire Mods are versatile fire resources that assist with prescribed fire preparation and execution, managing wildfires for resource benefit, fuels reduction work, wildfire response, etc.

Windfall/Windrow: Trees knocked over or broken off by the wind; also, sometimes called blowdown. Large areas of dense blowdown can create a serious fire hazard.

Work-to-Rest: A phrase that speaks to the amount of rest required for each hour worked. Current NWCG guidelines require one hour of rest for every two hours in work status. The average shift for a firefighter is 16 hours with 8 hours off.

Yard Sale: Generally, firefighters are pretty dialed, and organized because space is limited in vehicles, fire packs, etc. When a person has their stuff all over the place fellow firefighters refer to it as a yard sale and might offer them some money for a couple of their items just to give them a hard time.

Yellow: When a firefighter refers to their yellow, they are talking about their fire-resistant button-up fire shirt. Although fire shirts have been yellow for almost the entire history of wildland firefighting, there are fire shirts in other colors. Ironically, people still refer to their fire shirt as their "yellow" whether it's yellow or not.

AUTHORS

Tony Allabastro:
Bear Tango

Betty:
If You Give a Mouse a Chance

Downtown Sarah Brown:
Dirt Nap
Typical Night Shift

Riva Duncan:
Karma in an Oyster Tin
Find more from this author at:
www.rivaduncan.com

Steve Holdsambeck:
Bullwinkle

A. Taylor Johnson:
The Chetco Effect

Jumper 1:
Comin' in HOT

Bequi Livingston:
Binkies, Blankets, and Binoculars

Rikki Luebke:
Uncooked Poultry

Courtney McGee:
Perspective

TM:
June 27th

Caleb Miller:
Stitches

Milly:
Vienna Sausages

The Evolving Nomad:
Recipe for Camaraderie
Find more from this author at:
www.theevolvingnomad.com

Wally Ochoa+ Bre Orcasitas:
Having a Bit of a Fitbit

Bre Orcasitas:
The Legend of Ed Pulaski
Find more from this author at:
www.theevolvingnomad.com

AP:
The Unforgettables

Bobbie Scopa:
Dead Doug Fir
Find more from this author at:
www.bobbieonfire.com

Chris Surgenor:
Humility

Dee Townsend:
Bear Bait

ARTISTS

Anonymous:
The Incredible Floating Cubee
Best Spike Camp View
Fire Notebook

Tonja Opperman:
Aerial Recon
Captain's View
Firing Operations
Flare Up on the Fireline
Rock-N-Roll Crown Fire

She'll Survive
Flame
Find more from this artist at:
tonja-opperman.pixels.com

Stephanie Peters:
Crown Fire Smoke
Smoke in the Field
Winter Forest
Find more from this artist at:
https://www.stephartist.com

Sheena Waters:
The Scout
Initial Attack
Find more from this artist at:
@Scorchedelementdesigns (on IG)
Scorched Element Designs (on FB)

POETS

Emma Ruth Anderson:
Last Day of the Rodeo
We Celebrate Gorgeous
Find more from this artist at:
@emmaruths (on IG)

Andrew Foster Armstrong:
Nightly Comfort
A Belt Digs

Paul Keller:
The Bison and the Wildfire

Lookout Laura:
Haiku
Prose of Being a Lookout

Scan this QR code for information about how to make a submission for future volumes of *Hold and Improve,* or visit: *www.thevolvingnomad.com*

ACKNOWLEDGMENTS

A very sincere and heartfelt thank you goes out to these amazing humans:

James McGury- Thank you for trusting me enough to join me on this journey. I am in awe of your patience along the way as we essentially built a bicycle blindfolded. Your work is incredible, and truly appreciated.

Ian Morgan- Your capacity to continually support whatever seemingly wild thing my intuition drives me toward completely blows me away. Thank you for always giving me the space to do what I feel is right.

Ingram Content Group UK Ltd.
Milton Keynes UK
UKHW011947080523
421401UK00005B/558

9 780578 290362